Status and Dimensions of Grand Ayatollah Khamenei's Nuclear Fatwa from the Perspective of International Law

In the Name of God,

The most Beneficent, The most Merciful

Title: Nuclear Fatwa under International Law
Author: Jaber Seyvanizad
Subject: Public International Law
Size: 6" x 9" (15.24 x 22.86 cm)
Type: Black & White on White paper
Number of Pages: 250, Includes bibliographical references and index
Publisher: Supreme Century, RESEDA, CALIFORNIA, USA
ISBN-13: 978-1939123428
ISBN-10: 1939123429
Library of Congress Control Number (LCCN): 2017930601
Publication Date: 2017, printed in the United States of America

All rights reserved. No part of this book may be reprinted or reproduced or utilized in any form or by any electronic, mechanical, or other means, now known or hereafter invited, including photocopying and recoding, or in any information storage or retrieval system, without permission in writing from the author. For more information about permissions or to request permissions online, contact the author via e-mail: sayvania@ymail.com

Thanks to all those who helped
me in writing this book.....

Dedicated to:

Respectable opponents

In a joint press conference with German Chancellor Angela Merkel on Monday, President Obama said he believed a deal with Iran on nuclear weapons was possible because Supreme Leader Khamenei said it would be "contrary to their faith to obtain a nuclear weapon."

2015/02/09

Table of Contents

1). Word of the Author 23
2). Introduction 27
3). Importance and Necessity 28
4). Review of the Research Records 29
5). New Aspects and Innovation of Research 30
6). Research Purposes 31
7). Research Questions: 31
8). Research Hypotheses 32
9). Definition of Some Technical Words 33
10). Methods and Tools for Data Collection 33
11). Organization of Research 34
The Study on the Concept of Fatwa and a Governmental Decree 35
1.1. Literature Review 37
1.2. The System of Fatwa and its Fundamentals 39
1.2.1. The Reasons Study of Prohibition on WMD Use 41
1.2.1.1. Quran 41
1.2.1.1.1. The Implication of the Verse of E'tedah on Banning the Use of nuclear weapons 43
1.2.1.1.2. Comments of the Qur'an Commentators 44
1.2.1.2. Hadiths 45
1.2.2. Study of the Conceptual Indications of Some Hadiths on

Prohibition of Production and Usage of Nuclear Weapons 48
1.2.2.1. Some Supporting Implications: 48
1.2.3. Comments of Islamic Scholars on the Prohibition of Poisoning During War 49
1.2.4. Comments of Islamic Scholars on Incendiary Weapons 51
1.2.5. Islamic Scholars View about the Banning the Use of WMD 52
1.2.5.1. Shia Scholars 52
1.2.5.2. Sunni Scholars 53
1.2.5.2.3. Shafe'i Scholars 54
1.2.5.2.4. Hanbali Scholars 55
1.2.5.2.5. Maliki Scholars 55
1.3. Governmental Decree under Islamic Tenets 56
1.3.1. Relationships between Fatwa and Governmental Decree 56
1.3.2. Authenticity Reasons of Governmental Decree 58
1.3.3. Thematic Domain of Governmental Decree 59
1.4. Governmental Decree in the Iranian Constitution 60
1.4.1. Constitution and the Issuance Authority of Governmental Decree by the Supreme Leader 60
1.4.1.1. General Axes 61
1.4.1.2. Islamic Nature of System and Governmental Decree 61
1.4.1.3. Vilayateh Faqih and Governmental Decree 62
1.4.2. Some Constitutional Evidence for Authority and Authenticity of Leader's Governmental Decree. 63
1.4.2.1. Article (Principle) Hundred Ten: 63
1.4.2.2. Article Hundred Twelve 65
1.4.2.3. The Other Articles of Constitution 66
1.4.3. Legal Status of Governmental Decree under the Constitutional law of Islamic Republic of Iran 67
1.4.3.1. Governmental Decree of Valiyeh Faqih as One of the Sources of Constitutional law 67
1.4.3.2. Governmental Decree of Valiyeh Faqih, the Extraordinary Situations and Crisis 68
2.1. The Role of the Court in the Development of International law 76
2.1.1. Traditional Approach 77
2.1.2. Realistic Approach 77
2.2. Sources of Law of evidence Proving Claim in International Court

of Justice 80
2.2.1. Written Sources: 81
2.2.1.1. Principle Sources: 82
2.2.1.2. Secondary Sources: 83
2.2.2. Unwritten Sources:...85
2.2.2.1. General Principles of International law: 86
2.2.2.2. International Jurisprudence: 88
2.3. Principles Governing the Production, Admissibility and Evaluation of the Evidence in the International Court of Justice: 92
2.3.1. Principles Governing the Process of Fact-finding in International Court of Justice: 93
2.3.1.1. The Parties Freedom to Produce Evidence: 94
2.3.1.2. Court Freedom to Accept and Evaluate Evidence:.................94
2.4. Statements by Officials or Governmental Institutions: 95
2.5. Guiding Principles Applicable to Unilateral 107
2.5.1. Guiding Principles Applicable to Unilateral Declarations of States Capable of Creating Legal Obligations, with Commentaries thereto 2006..109
3.1. Generalities 129
3.2. Definition of International Custom: 132
3.3. Material Element:..133
3.3.1. The Practice Makers, ...133
3.3.1.1. States: 133
3.3.1.2. International Organizations: 138
3.3.1.3. International Judicial Authorities: 141
3.3.1.4. Non-governmental International Organizations:...................143
3.3.2. Nature of Practice:..146
3.3.2.1. Verbal and Material Acts: 146
3.3.2.2. Verbal Element; Emergence in the Practice or Legal Belief?152
3.3.2.3. Refusal or Omission: 154
3.3.3. Characteristics of the Practice: 156
3.3.3.1. The Generality of Practice and the Limits of This Generality:157
3.3.3.2. The Time Element: 158
3.3.3.3. Integrity and Uniformity of Practices: 160
3.3.3.4. The Practice of the Beneficiary States: 162
3.4.1. Concept and Necessity 163

3.4.1.1. Concept 163
3.4.1.2. Necessity 164
3.4.2. Nature 165
3.4.2.1. The Consent Theory of the Voluntarist.................................166
3.4.2.2. Legal Beliefs Derived From the Necessities...........................167
3.4.3. Status of the Principles and Fundamental Rules.......................168
3.5. The Recognition of a Customary Law with Relying on the Central Role of Legal Belief...170
3.5.1. Recognition of the Concept and Review of Some Theoretical Concepts: 170
3.5.1.1. Concept and Origin: 170
3.5.1.2. Theoretical Fundamentals: 174
3.5.2. The Procedure of the International "Judicial Practice":............180
3.5.2.1. International Court of Justice:..180
3.6. Comparative Study of Fatwa Sui Generis with N.P.T and the Advisory Opinion of International Court of Justice:.........................184
3.6.1. Generalities:..184
3.6.3. The Superiority of Fatwa to the System of Treaties 189
3.6.4. The Legality of Threat or Use of Nuclear Weapons: 192
3.6.5. Conclusions 197
3.6.7. Bibliography...204
3.6.8. Appendixes 221
3.6.9. Index 248

LIST OF ABBREVIATIONS

AJIL	American Journal of International Law
BILC	British International Cases
BYIL	British Yearbook of International Law
CathULRev	Catholic University Law Review
ChiJIntlL	Chicago Journal of International Law
CornellIntlLJ	Cornell International Law Journal
CUP	Cambridge University Press
EJIL	European Journal of International Law
EuZW	Europäische Zeitschrift für Wirtschaftsrecht
FYBIL	Finnish Yearbook of International Law
FordhamIntlLJ	Fordham International Law Journal
GYIL	German Yearbook of International Law
HagueYIL	Hague Yearbook of International Law
HarvIntlLJ	Harvard International Law Journal

HousJIntlL	Houston Journal of International Law
ICLQ	International and Comparative Law Quarterly
IJIL	Indian Journal of International Law
ILR	International Law Reports
JC&SL	Journal of Conflict and Security Law
JIntL&Prac	Journal of International Law and Practice
JIntlArb	Journal of International Arbitration
LJIL	Leiden Journal of International Law
NCLRev	North Carolina Law Review
NSAIL	Non-State Actors and International Law
OJLS	Oxford Journal of Legal Studies
PYIL	Polish Yearbook of International Law
REDI	Revista Española de Derecho Internacional
SpanYIL	Spanish Yearbook of International Law
StanJIntlL	Stanford Journal of International Law
TexIntlLJ	Texas International Law Journal
UChiLRev	University of Chicago Law Review
UFlaLRev	University of Florida Law Review
UNYB	Yearbook of the United Nations
UNYBILC	Yearbook of the International Law Commission
VaJIntlL	Virginia Journal of International Law
WisIntlLJ	Wisconsin International Law Journal
WldAff	World Affairs
YaleJIntlL	Yale Journal of International Law
HJIL	Heidelberg Journal of International Law

Glossary

Ab Initio: from the start; from the beginning.
Accusare Nemo Se Debet Nisi Coram Deo: no man is obliged to accuse himself except before God.
Acta Exteriora Indicant Interiora Secreta: the outward acts show the secret intentions.
Actio Personalis Moritur Cum Persona: any right of action dies with the person.
Actus Dei Nemini Facit Injuriam: an act of God causes legal injury to no one.
Actus Reus: a prohibited act.
Ad Hoc: limited in time; to this point.
Ad Infinitum: forever; without limit; indefinitely.

Ad Proximum Antecedens Fiat Relatio Nisi Impediatur Sententia: relative words must ordinarily be referred to the last antecedent, the last antecedent being the last word which can be made an antecedent so as to give a meaning.

Ad Referendum: for further consideration by one having the authority to make a final decision

Alieni Juris: under the legal authority of another.

Animus: intention.

Bona Fide: good faith.

Boni Judicis Est Ampliare Jurisdictionem: good justice is broad jurisdiction.

Casus Foederis: treaty event.

Ceteris Paribus: all things being equal or unchanged.

Communis Error Facit Jus: common error makes right.

Consensus Ad Idem: a meeting of the minds.

Consensus Tollit Errorem: consent obviates errors in the course of judicial proceedings.

Consuetudo Volentes Ducit, Lex Nolentes Trahit: customs leads the willing, law drags the unwilling.

Cursus Curiae Est Lex Curiae: the practice of the court is the law of the court.

De Novo: new.

De facto: in reality

De Jure: according to law

Dicta or Dictum: saying.

Ejusdem or Eiusdem Generis: of the same kind or nature.

Erga Omnes rules: towards everyone

Et. al.: and others.

Ex Aequo Et Bono: in justice and fairness.

Ex Debito Justitiae: as of right.

Ex Juris: outside of the jurisdiction.

Expressio Unius Est Exclusio Alterius: the expression of one thing is the exclusion of the other.

Fetiales: type of priest in Ancient Rome
Hostis Humani Generis: the enemy of mankind.
Ignorantia Juris Non Excusat: ignorance of the law is no excuse.
In Fictione Juris Semper Aequitas Existit: with legal fictions, equity always exists.
In haec verba: verbatim.
In Jure Non Remota Causa Sed Proxima Spectatur: in law the near cause is looked to, not the remote one.
In Limine: at the beginning or on the threshold.
Inter Alia: 'among other things', 'for example' or 'including'.
Inter Partes: between, among parties.
Interpretatio Cessat in Claris: interpretation stops when a text is clear.
Inter Se: as between or amongst themselves.
In Tota Fine Erga Omnes Et Omnia: for all purposes, in regards to all and everything.
Ipso Facto: by the act itself.
Ipso Jure: by operation of law.
Jura Regalia: by right, under legal authority.
Jure: the law or a legal right.
Jus Ad Bellum: the legal authority to wage war.
Jus Civile: civil law
Jus Cogens: peremptory law.
Jus Dispositivum: law adopted by consent.
Jus Gentium: law of the nations
Jus Sanguinis: right of blood
Jus Soli: right of soil (land)
Jus Transitas Innoxii: right of safe passage
Jus Ex Injuria Non Oritur: a legal right or entitlement cannot arise from an unlawful act or omission.
Jus Vitae Necisque: power of life and death.
Leges Posteriores Priores Contrarias Abrogant: later laws abrogate prior contrary laws.

Lex Non Scripta: unwritten law; the common or custom law.
Lex Non Scripta, Diuturni Mores Consensus Utensium Comprobati: law derived from custom must be firmly entrenched in practice and adopted and followed by tradition.
Mala Fides: bad faith
Malum In Se: something wrong in itself.
Malum prohibitum: wrong because prohibited.
Non Liquet: a situation where there is no applicable law.
Noscitur A Sociis: that the meaning of a word may be known from accompanying words.
Omne Majus Continet In Se Minus: the greater contains the less.
Pacta Sunt Servanda: agreements must be kept.
Per Se: of itself.
Persona Non Grata: person not appreciated
Prima Facie: a legal presumption which means on the face of it or at first sight.
Pro Bono: for the good.
Pro Se: on one's own behalf.
Pro Tempore: something done temporarily only and not intended to be permanent.
Quando Jus Domini Regis Et Subditi Concurrunt, Jus Regis Praeferri Debet: when the right of the sovereign and that of a subject conflict, the right of the sovereign is to be preferred.
Quantum: amount or extent.
Quicquid Plantatur Solo, Solo Cedit: whatever is planted in the ground, belongs to the ground.
Quid Pro Quo: something for something.
Raison D'etre: forming cause of something.
Ratio Decidendi: reasons for a decision.
Rebus Sic Stantibus: changed circumstances.
Res Gestae: things done.
Res Communis: public domain and common heritage of mankind.
Respondeat Superior: let the principal answer.

Restitutio In Integrum: restitution to the original position.
Res Nullius: nobody's property
Se Defendendo: self-defence.
Sine Qua Non: without which, not.
Status Quo: the current situation
Sub Judice: under judicial consideration.
Sui Generis: of its own kind.
Sui Juris: one's own law; having full capacity.
Summa Ratio Est Quae Pro Religione Facit: the best rule is that which advances religion.
Ubi Eadem Ratio, Ibi Idem Jus: where there is the same reason, there is the same law
Ultra Petita: beyond that which is sought.
Use: trust.
Uti Possidetis: as you possess
Utile Per Inutile Non Vitiatur: that which is useful is not vitiated by that which is useless.
Valeat Quantum Valere Potest: it shall have effect as far as it can have effect.
Vinculum Juris: a legal bound.

Abstract

The Issuance of the nuclear Fatwa, by grand Ayatollah Sayed Ali Khamenei, as a significant basis for the subjects of international law, is considered as a founder of a new period in Iran's legal relations , particularly in the route of nuclear talks with (5 + 1). In this regard, growing welcome of international officials in public acceptance of nuclear Fatwa has been evident and remarkable. This religious order in status of an authentic international document, not only creates inviolable international obligations, but beyond that, shapes a new discourse in the literature of international relations and law as well. The legal regime of the nuclear Fatwa is positioned in a more comprehensive and effective status in comparison with Non-proliferation Treaty, insofar as contrary to the Treaty, in this legal regime there is no any discrimination between nuclear weapon States and non-nuclear weapon States in use, production and stockpiling of weapons of mass destruction. This research has been conducted in a qualitative meta-analysis method. The results indicate that the initial steps taken towards the creation of a new international custom emanating from nuclear Fatwa are aimed to achieve sustainable international peace and security with a new justice-based approach.

Keywords: Nuclear Fatwa, International Authenticity, International Custom, Non- Proliferation Treaty

1). Word of the Author

Some important factors prompted the writing of this book, insofar as if they had not been, this research would have not been done. They are classified into two groups. First, factors which encouraged the writer to conduct this research and second, factors that were raison d'être of this research. In describing the first group, since the issuance of nuclear Fatwa, some critics tried to deny the existence of this Fatwa, in spite of its public manifestation by the Supreme Leader in several occasions, and also by Iran's foreign ministry.

Even after the documentation of nuclear Fatwa as an international act in United Nations, some critics continued their previous position in denying the existence of nuclear Fatwa[1]. For years these critics did not change such a position. It was interesting that President Obama recognized nuclear Fatwa and repeatedly

---

1. See http://www.cnsnews.com/news/article/patrick-goodenough/, http://www.tabletmag.com/jewish-news-and-politics/97762/irans-missing-nuclear-fatwa,http://blog.camera.org/archives/2015/04/fatwa_what_fatwa_does_ayatolla_1.html,http://www.nationalreview.com/corner/417043/,http://freebeacon.com/national-security/research-organization-disputes-existence-of-anti-nuke-fatwa/,http://www.dailymail.co.uk/news/article-2439490/Middle-East-research-group-Irans-fatwa-nukes-cited-Obama-twice-week-doesnt-exist.html,http://www.usatoday.com/story/news/world/2013/10/04/iran-fatwa-nuclear-weapons/2922517/

uttered it, at least as a legally meaningful base, but more Catholic than pope did not. Nevertheless, as various States began to accept the nuclear Fatwa, the continuation of denial policy was very hard.

Accordingly, they[1] replaced the policy of falsification with the policy of denial. In this phase of operation against the nuclear Fatwa first they attempted to challenge its religious nature by resorting to Islamic principle of "Taqiyyeh". Every Islamic expert knows that this Principle is completely irrelevant to nuclear Fatwa, because "Taqiyyeh" is a principle which is applicable only in case of fear, whereas nuclear Fatwa was issued from the position of strength, not weakness. This fact that one State is able to produce nuclear weapons, and does not do it because of its long standing policies, absolutely comes from the position of strength. Hence, this misgiving quickly lost its utility as well.

In the next round of misgivings, some critics tried to challenge the longevity of the nuclear Fatwa, and posed this question whether it is changeable overnight or not? Even though this question was in line with the other attempts, it deserved more to be answered. The comprehensive recognition of various layers of the nuclear Fatwa can be effective in responding to such a question. As discussed more in parts of the book, the domestic legal status of nuclear Fatwa is definable in two levels; religious level and governmental level, whether the vote can be changed or not, only relates to the religious level, because Iran's government is based on religion. On this basis, we should discover the exact position of Fatwa under Islam generally, and Shia jurisprudence specifically. In short, the nuclear Fatwa, as it will be discussed, is a primary governmental edict and, because of such a nature, is permanently unchangeable.

---

1. In this respect, see: Nuclear Fatwa, Religion and Politics in Iran's Proliferation Strategy, Michael Eisenstadt and Mehdi Khalaji, Published in 2011 in the United States of America by The Washington Institute for Near East Policy ,September 2011

Some critics,[1] referring to remarks of Mr. Mosavian -one of negotiators of IRI in case of Salman Rushdie-, try to have the same perception toward both Fatwas. In that case, the Iranian side, in order to persuade the western side, declared that, Imam's Fatwa is not something forever and in case of Salman Rushdie's repentance is changeable. But the nature of nuclear Fatwa is completely different, because what Imam issued was a secondary governmental edict, and what Ayatollah Khamenei has issued is a primary governmental edict. In other words, the type of Fatwas is different, and consequently their functions and mechanisms vary. However, Imam's Fatwa in prohibition of chemical weapons has a similar nature with nuclear Fatwa and because of that, it is also unchangeable. Responding to these baseless misgivings was my chief motivation. It should be noted that the better explanation of nuclear Fatwa and responding to misgivings, even about those that are irrelevant, will be useful in recognition of nuclear Fatwa's Status under international law.

The second group that is called this research's raison d'être include the confirmation of the nuclear Fatwa by the highest international officials, especially President Obama, and also its documentation as an international act in United Nations. Finally, the other important factor of this kind is the 1945 Truman Proclamation relating to the right to explore and exploit resources of the sea bed. The registration of nuclear Fatwa in United Nations ended all doubts relating to the existence of the Fatwa. The confirmation of the nuclear Fatwa by international officials, including president Obama, not only eliminated many fabricated challenges against the nuclear Fatwa but also guaranteed its legal life in its evolutionary process. And Truman proclamation showed that an international unilateral act has this capability to be custom-

---

1. see: to Be or not to Be, Fact and Fiction in the Nuclear Fatwa Debate ,Ali M. Ansari, University of St. Andrews, February 2013,?

maker under international law, so why not about the nuclear Fatwa –which enjoys the same legal personality-?

Finally I prefer to address few points. I observe IRI's actions in international community neutrally, as I would observe those of any other State; agreeing with some, and opposing others. I definitely have never received a penny from the Iranian governmental sources on matters concerning this research. I value my independence and dignity as a legal scholar above everything else in my academic life. One of the notable reasons I continue to write in this area is that there are few independent, university-based international jurists writing on international law issues, in particular, topic of Iran's nuclear program -specifically nuclear fatwa-, and I think that it is significant to have independent voices assessing the legal disputes of the States parties to this conflict, as in any other subcategories of international law. From the other side, for meticulously commenting on the multi-layered aspects of nuclear fatwa, a researcher needs to be equipped to the knowledge of Islamic law on one hand and the knowledge of international and constitutional law simultaneously on the other. Since the same researches conducted in this respect don't enjoy the aforesaid privilege, the current research with the above-mentioned qualifications, presents a legally unique investigation and methodologically distinguishes itself. In the second chapter, the references to the literature on unilateral acts of States seems to be inadequate and author has provided a short legal explanation at the end of each article. Since some topics in the first chapter overlaps with some others in the second, retelling them in the second section has been avoided.

Within the chapter three and forth, author has comprehensively addressed the procedures before the International Court of Justice, sources of international law and the nature of Customary international law. One may think that this extent of analysis may be unnecessary or superfluous especially with regard to the primary topic concerning the Fatwa Status. Logically when we want to analyze the quality of fatwa from the perspective of international law subcategories first we have to determine the geography of discussion in detail. In this case, readers easily can perceive the thematic correlation of issues with each other and any kind of explanation remarkably guides them for much better perception. In this study reader deeply needs to understand the relation of issues step by step and this is why we addressed the jurisprudence of ICJ and other international tribunals to prove first the authenticity of referring to ICJ judgments and then extension of its inclusion circle to the subject of Fatwa. For example, in argument concerning the customary international law, without addressing the two-fold nature of CIL and analyzing it, one may challenge our deduction towards the custom-maker capability of nuclear fatwa. Whereas if his mind had been adequately warmed up, he or she could have easily devoured it.

At the end, it must be noted that the current book has been written by a middle-eastern young jurist and in terms of English standards there may be some defects and lack of fluency. However, employing an unpretentious language, author has tried to simply convey his message to his audience.

2). Introduction

The edict known as "nuclear Fatwa" issued by the Supreme Leader of Iran, created a new chapter among the international law think tanks, and generally among the international centers for the strategic studies; because firstly, this Fatwa is in line with the ultimate goal of international law[1] which is to maintain the international peace and security. Also, in terms of being a Fatwa is binding for large groups of Muslims, and in terms of edict, is in place of an inflexible and imperative rule for Iranian authorities.

---

1. UN charter, article 1

Iran, as a State that, according to Western politicians, is always away with some international norms, and as a result, this peculiarity has reduced the level of its relationships, especially with Western countries, transmitted a message from itself that could increasingly attract, perhaps for the first time the attention of the elite politicians and western States officials, in a way that they supported it in world official tribunes. This is considered as an unprecedented adaptive point between Iran and West after the 1979 Islamic revolution in Iran; and was realized when Supreme Leader's Fatwa was issued in prohibition of production, usage and stockpiling of nuclear weapons. The increasing welcoming atmosphere to the Fatwa among the world political and official authorities on the one hand and, various theorizations of the international law thinkers in academic circles on the other, and of course misinterpretations of some others prompted the writer to explain the status and multiple dimensions of this document with a comprehensive and legal approach by the way of the international law imperatives.

3). Importance and Necessity

The importance of recognizing the international aspects of this Fatwa under international law, is that, this Fatwa prohibits the use, proliferation and stockpiling of a weapon that is the biggest threat against international peace and security from the perspective of international law. Therefore, recognizing the concepts and highlighting the hidden security values in this source, along with mentioning the international law views, reduce the threats and will be influential in the realization of the global security process. Moreover, a methodical study in this field, for the first time, can be an effective step towards the international recognition of Fatwa in order not to be misinterpreted. Using the capacity of the Fatwa in the creation of an international consensus relating to the maintenance of international justice-based peace and security, doubles its importance. Because based on international law, it enjoys legal Status and international authenticity, the practice-making provenance of the nuclear Fatwa, at least in relation to the non-proliferation policy, can be a harbinger to create regional, extra-regional, and in a bigger realm, universal custom. For example, a State like USA benefited from the theories of preventive and preemptive wars in Iraq and Afghanistan war, which have no inviolable position under international law, UN Charter and other international documents, and instead, enjoyed merely some theoretical supports. Nevertheless, how can the outcome of peace and security derived from the legal regime of nuclear Fatwa be easily ignored?

4). Review of the Research Records

In connection with the nuclear Fatwa, so far, several studies in various regional and global levels have been conducted, mostly in terms of politics. Therefore, since the current study analyzes this issue from the perspective of international law, according to the content, the advantage of domestic and foreign legal sources is used. Some of which are mentioned as follows:

Number of Domestic Studies:

Zanjani, 2001, in a study entitled "Political Jurisprudence" believes that the governmental decree is one of the authentic sources of the Islamic jurisprudence which holds the political aspects.

Tavakkol, 2009, in a study entitled "Legal Study of Iran's Nuclear Program" believes that, IAEA has cited Iranian official statements.

Zamani, 2006, in his book entitled "Collection of International Instruments on Human Rights" states that, not using the W.M.D is one of the inviolable principles of international instruments on human rights.

Khalili, 2011, in his book entitled "Governmental Decrees" believes that the primary governmental edicts issued by the supreme leader are permanently irreversible

Mir Abbasi, 2010, in a study entitled "International proceedings" believes that the official statements are authentic under international law, and referable in international tribunals.

Number of Foreign Studies:

M. Ansari, 2013, Netherlands, in the research of "To be or not to be fact and fiction in the nuclear Fatwa debate", believes that the nuclear Fatwa, in spite of being remarkable from the perspective of international law, is completely challengeable.

Tabatabai, 2012, London, in the research of "Don't misunderstand Khamenei's nuclear Fatwa", believes that the authenticity of this document is questionable.

Mousavian, 2013, USA, in the article of "Globalizing Iran's Fatwa against nuclear weapon", defends the statements of Iran's supreme leader and the validity of his Fatwa.

Rifkind, Ingram, Sadeghi-Boroujerdi, 2012, London, in the research of "Iran's nuclear impasse: Breaking the deadlock", states that: this Fatwa is one of the subsidiary sources of the international law.

Joyner, 2013, USA, in the article of "International lawifying the supreme leader's Fatwa", believes that: this Fatwa is an authentic document under the international law.

5). New Aspects and Innovation of Research

The nuclear Fatwa, in terms of international relations and political science norms, has been superficially and repeatedly studied, however, it has not been analyzed meticulously under the international law view and its subcategories. Hence, the current research is considered as a noble study in terms of research style and its international law approach.

6). Research Purposes

The purpose of the present research is to investigate the viewpoint of the international law with all its headings associated with various elements of the nuclear Fatwa that will be available by a general classification to the position and dimensions of the (nuclear Fatwa) under the international law. On this basis, various components of Fatwa will be studied one by one with all related headings of international law separately, and they will be compared and recognized in terms of their matching or contrasting points, or any other possible relationships.

Even though the study is not supported by any organization or institute, its results will have some tangible effects, insofar as its theorization can internationally recognize the new unknown horizons in the realm of international law.

7). Research Questions:

Main Questions

1). Can the nuclear Fatwa be considered as an international act? And in case of its authentication, is it considered as one example of the law of evidence proving claim before the international tribunals?

2). Can nuclear Fatwa be considered as one of the sources of international law? (at least regarding its formally documentation in UN, as a subsidiary tool and in the form of a preparatory act in recognition of international law sources).

Subsidiary Questions

1). Are the legal elements of Fatwa in the same direction with the purpose and sources of international law?

2). What is the difference between the issuance of Fatwa and a governmental decree by the supreme leader?

3). With regard to Imam Khomeini's Fatwa in prohibition of chemical weapons and the other international authentic Fatwas issued by Valiyeh Faqihs, can it be considered as an international Islamic norm?

8). Research Hypotheses

Main Hypotheses

1). Nuclear Fatwa is not a one-dimensional document that contains merely the religious aspects, all aspects and its legal originality must be considered together. Nuclear Fatwa as an internationally unilateral act is referable before the international tribunals.

2). According to article 38 of ICJ Statute and advisory opinion of ILC concerning the recognition of the judicial decisions and the teachings of the most highly qualified publicists of the various nations, as subsidiary means for the determination of rules of law, nuclear Fatwa also can be considered as one of the aforementioned subsidiary means.

Subsidiary Hypotheses

1). Nuclear Fatwa is consistent with all fundamentals, principles and purposes of international law including: articles of UN Charter, International covenant on civil and political rights, universal declaration of human rights, foursome treaties of Geneva, customary rules and other sources of international law.

2). The issued decree by Valiyeh Faqih enjoys a legal nature and is binding for all pillars and components of the country, whereas Fatwa does not enjoy such a function.

3). With regard to element of "repetition" on Fatwas of Imam

Khomeini and Ayatollah Khamenei in the prohibition of WMD, it can be concluded that such international Fatwas, depending on circumstances, are considered as a norm of the Islamic international law.

9). Definition of Some Technical Words

Governmental Decree: is a title for some edicts of Valiyeh Faqih which mostly holds an extrajudicial nature, but that is binding for all based on the expression stipulation of absolute authority in Constitution. (Khalili, 2011, p27)

Fatwa: means the explanation of Allah's ruling by Faqih. (Khalili, 2011, p25)

Weapons of Mass Destruction: are weapons that can kill many humans and cause lots of damages to infrastructures and environments. (Momtaz, 2011, p14)

Unilateral Declaration: is an internationally legal act which is issued by a State and usually makes the issuing state committed to some commitments. (Watts, 1999)

Non-proliferation Treaty: the treaty whereby, 188 member-state, committed to non-proliferation of their nuclear weapon and also not leaving their knowledge at the other states disposal in order to achieve nuclear weapons.

10). Methods and Tools for Data Collection

In this study, the library method has been used. Some internet databases, books and English journals have been used in order to obtain the scientific literature and history of research. Also based on necessities, some domestic and international rules including, Constitution, UN Charter, Conventions and the other sources of international law have been cited.

11). Organization of Research

This study is composed of three chapters. In the first chapter we explore the nature of a Fatwa and a governmental decree. In the second chapter we speak about the authenticity of Fatwa based on law case of ICJ and 2006 guiding principles of ILC. In the last chapter we analyze the custom-making process of the legal regime[1] of the nuclear Fatwa and its comparative study with N.P.T and finally by a general conclusion, present some suggestions.

---

1. A legal regime is a system of principles and rules governing something, and which is created by law. It is framework of legal rules. (http://definitions.uslegal.com/l/legal-regime). Accordingly, use of combination of legal regime for the legal institution of Fatwa is correct. Firstly this Fatwa contains the general principles and rules governing on weapons of mass destruction. Secondly, based on definition, relates to a specific issue. Thirdly has been made from the primary Islamic rules and principles of Constitution and finally, is considered as a general framework for lawmaking process concerning weapons of mass destruction. (Seivanizad, 2013)

Chapter One

The Study on the Concept of Fatwa and a Governmental Decree

1.1. Literature Review

For the first time, grand Ayatollah Khamenei, disclosed his opinion about the nuclear weapons in Imam Reza's shrine in 2003, when he said: "We are not interested in nuclear weapons. We are against the chemical weapons. Such things are against our principles"[1] (Khamenei, 2003). During that year, he repeatedly spoke about the prohibition of WMD under divine legal logic and said: "We are basically, logically and fundamentally against the WMD. During the imposed war against Iran also, we prohibited the biologic and chemical weapons."(Khamenei, 2003)

Ayatollah Khamenei brought a religious reason for banning the nuclear weapons, for the first time. Based on the religious nature of Iran's State, presentation of some bizarre comments by Islamic Scholars is not unavailable. Accordingly, some Islamic experts, unlike the main stream, were persisting in the preventive aspect of nuclear weapon sporadically. On this basis, the supreme leader who is the best one in religious affairs, and the last decision maker at the top of State declared, formally, Iran's State policy about the WMD.

---

1. Available at: http://islam-pure.de/imam/speeches/speech2003.htm.

During several speeches he promulgated this policy. In a political meeting he said: "Islamic Republic of Iran, based on its fundamental religious and legal beliefs, never resorts to WMD. Unlike the enemies' propaganda, we basically disagree with the production of WMD."(Khamenei, 2003) This policy of the supreme leader institutionalized within Iran's administrative system insofar as, the nuclear prohibition was imparted to several military and research units as a circular.

Dr. Hassan Rouhani, the Iranian time secretary of Supreme Council of National Security declared repeatedly there is no any guarantee proving peacefulness of Iran's nuclear activities, more important than the supreme leader's Fatwa prohibiting the production, use and stockpiling of WMD. Dr. Rouhani, in his meeting with the foreign ministers of France, Germany and England, introduces the Nuclear Fatwa as a document which is more important than N.P.T, and the additional protocol. Francois Nicoullaud, ambassador of France in Iran says," Dr. Rouhani sent the circular of the nuclear Fatwa to all ministries and entities of the system, including military and non-military institutions, and asked them to report all their related activities since the beginning to now[1]. (Porter, 2013)

Since 2003, Ayatollah Khamenei repeatedly addressed the western States, and proclaimed Iran's peaceful policy in relation to nuclear activities. The Nuclear Fatwa was registered in United Nations and also among the documents of IAEA as an international act and also was considered as a meaningful base for the nuclear disarmament talks in Tehran's disarmament Conference. With regard to the twofold nature of nuclear Fatwa, in checking its international authenticity, first we must segregate these two dimensions, then analyze each of them separately; on this basis, the primary dimension includes the religious aspect, and

---

1. Rouhani›s interview with Mehrnameh magazine, 2011.

the secondary dimension contains its governmental aspect.

1.2. The System of Fatwa and its Fundamentals

In order to make religious inferences of the rule about the utilization of nuclear weapon, a Faqih[1] must give priority to recognition of subject (nuclear weapon). Because if someone doesn't know what a nuclear bomb is, how its destructive effects are, what its radius of the adverse and disastrous influences in length and width of human life is, what effects will it have on the next generations, and how many people annihilate in the time of explosion; basically cannot deduce and present a correct result from Islamic sources[2].

A nuclear weapon is different from conventional weapons; destructs environment and also has destructive effects on human life and human genetic and generation. Today, after years of Hiroshima nuclear explosion, it can be seen that its disastrous effect has still remained, and now we know that when uranium is used even in a weakened scale, it has lots of destructive effects, and generally the production of these weapons jeopardizes the international security. Hence, consideration of the human and moral principles in production of weapons -that is, how much destructive weapon can be produced? - are the issues that must be scrutinized by Faqih in issuance of Fatwa.

For the issuance of a Fatwa, a Mujtahid first must seek Ijtidadi reason to determine related rule governing on the subject, and in case of lack of Ijtihadi reason, and emergence of doubt has to seek the Fiqahati reason including the principles: Isteshab, Baraat,

---

1. An expert in Islamic knowledge specifically in Islamic multi-layered rules.
2. "An Investigation of the Judicial Decree Regarding the Use of Nuclear Weapons in Jurisprudence and International law", Seyyed Javad Mirmahdipour Kouhkamari, 2014.

Ihtiyat and Takhyeer (Sheikhe Ansari, 1989, p315).The issue of banning the use of nuclear weapons in terms of abundance of banning reasons in Islamic texts including: Quran, Hadiths, Sunnah and Consensus indicating the expressions of the infallible Imams, the subject has the verbal frequency in the sources , i.e. there are too many reasons in the religious school of Sunnis and Shias collectively indicating the prohibition of the use of nuclear weapon. In this section a great number of those reasons will be analyzed and there is no any need to present the Fiqahati principle and reasons.

Of course, having the power and enjoyment of divine possibilities in case of non-violating someone's right is permitted, and too much evidence indicate its permission under the tenets derived from Quran, Hadiths and Reason, like the verse stating: "He it is Who created for you all that is on earth. Then He Istawa (rose over) towards the heaven and made them seven heavens and He is the All-Knower of everything" [1](Baqarah, 28). The energy resources are for all human beings and this is the right of nations to utilize these God-given blessings, and in this respect, no one has to be allowed by the other one. Also the other verses state that: "And surely, we gave you authority on the earth and appointed for you therein provisions (for your life). Little thanks do you give"[2] (A'raf, 10) or "And has subjected to you all that is in the heavens and all that is in the earth; it is all as a favour and kindness from Him. Verily, in it are signs for a people who think deeply [3]"(Jathiya, 13).

The issue of equipping a weapon for defending the country is rationally and religiously indispensable, and on this basis Imam Khomeini considers it as a State task (Khomeini, 1983, 23) and

---

1. هُوَ الَّذى خَلَقَ لَكُم مَا فى الأَرض جَميعا
2. وَلَقَد مَكَّنَّاكم فى الأَرض و جَعَلنا لَكُم فيها مَعايش
3. وسخَّر لكُم ما فى السَماوات و مافى الارض جميعا

this Khomeini's view is supported by many Islamic tenets. For example based on the verse stating: "And make ready against them all you can of power, including steeds of war to threaten the enemy of Allah and your enemy, and others besides whom, you may not know but whom Allah does know"[1](Anfal, 60). All Muslims must appear powerful before enemies, but the content of this verse must be scrutinized to be specified on its limits. The purpose of having weapons is creating fear among the enemies and this is the subject of the aforementioned verse. The verse has not stated you can use any evilness and rascality to threaten your enemy. When we proved nuclear weapon is not from instances of power, rather instances of evilness and brutality, it does not turn to talk of having it. Such things like having nuclear, biological and chemical weapons are out of instances of this verse.

In Hadiths and under the Sunnah, emphasis on equipment and having science and power in favor of peaceful and divine purposes is because of encouraging them (enemies) to give up their evilness. Human is perfectionist inherently and enjoyment of material powers can be defined under this process. Hence, enjoying the peaceful nuclear energy under the international law provisions is legal and permitted.

1.2.1. The Reasons Study of Prohibition on WMD Use

1.2.1.1. Quran

1. The verses indicate the prohibition of homicide, such as:" Because of that We ordained for the Children of Israel that if anyone killed a person not in retaliation of murder, or (and) to spread mischief in the land - it would be as if he killed all mankind, and if anyone saved a life, it would be as if he saved the life of all

---

1. وَأَعِدُّوا لَهُم مَّا اسْتَطَعْتُم مِّن قُوَّةٍ

mankind" [1](Ma'idah, 32) and "No person earns any (sin) except against himself (only), and no bearer of burdens shall bear the burden of another"[2]. (An'am, 164) The first verse indicates killing an innocent one before divine system is considered as killing all humans, so absolutely killing inhabitants of a city or country in which live many innocents is very heinous act before God. The second verse indicates no one must be victimized by other one's sin and everybody is responsible for his behaviors.

2. The verse introduces the destruction of generations and cities as the clear instances of corruption on the earth which is the minimum damage of nuclear armaments; "And when he turns away (from you "O Muhammad "), his effort in the land is to make mischief therein and to destroy the crops and the cattle, and Allah likes not mischief"[3] (Baqarah, 205)

3. The verse that prohibits the absolute domination on atheists; "Except those who join a group, between you and whom there is a treaty (of peace), or those who approach you with their breasts restraining from fighting you as well as fighting their own people. Had Allah willed, indeed He would have given them power over you, and they would have fought you. So if they withdraw from you, and fight not against you, and offer you peace, then Allah has opened no way for you against them" [4](Nisa', 90) expressing after ceasefire, Muslims do not have the right to refight against their enemy and take some concessions, hence when taking concessions from the enemy is invalid, how is it possible to kill innocent civilians who never interfered in war?

4. The verse that prohibits killing innocents; "and kill not anyone

---

1. مَن قَتَلَ نَفْساً بِغَيْرِ نَفْسٍ أَو فِسادٍ فِى الأَرضِ فَكَأَنَّما قَتَلَ النّاسَ جَميعًا
2. ولاتَزِر وازِرةٌ وِزرَ أُخرى
3. اذا تَوَلّى سَعى فِى الأَرضِ لِيُفسِدَ فيها ويُهلِكَ الحَرثَ و النَسلَ و اللهِ لايُحِبُّ الفَساد
4. فَإِنِ اعتَزَلوكُم فَلَم يُقاتِلوكُم و أَلقَوا إِلَيكُمُ السَلَمَ فَما جَعَلَ اللهُ لَكُم عَلَيهِم سَبيلا

whom Allah has forbidden, except for a just cause"[1] (An'am, 151).

5. The verse expressing the proportionality in punishments; "The sacred month is for the sacred month, and for the prohibited things, there is the Law of Equality (Qisas). Then whoever transgresses the prohibition against you, you transgress likewise against him. And fear Allah, and know that Allah is with Al-Muttaqun (the pious)"[2] (Baqarah, 194).

6. The verse forbidding the committing evils; "he commands them for Al-Ma'ruf (, i.e. Islamic Monotheism and all that Islam has ordained); and forbids them from Al-Munkar (, i.e. disbelief, polytheism of all kinds, and all that Islam has forbidden)"[3] (A'raf, 157). The clear example of "evil" which has been prohibited in verses and Hadiths obviously can be this one, and if supposed to be examples for "forbidding the evil", this one is definitely one of them.

7. The verse emphasizing on criminal justice and referring to principle of distinction; "And fight in the Way of Allah those who fight you, but transgress not the limits. Truly, Allah likes not the transgressors" [4](Baqarah, 190)[5]

1.2.1.1.1. The Implication of the Verse of E'tedah on Banning the Use of nuclear weapons

The verse 190 the Sura of Baqarah is one of the most significant verses related to the prohibition of WMD use, because some principles and general rules of war are extractable by it, including:

A). Principle of Proportionality in War Armaments

---

1. ولاَ تَقْتُلُ النَفْسَ التى حَرَّمَ اللهُ الا بِالْحَقِ
2. فَمَن اعتَدا عَلَيكُم اعتَدوا علَيه بِمِثل ما اعتَدى عَلَيكُم واتَّقواللهَ واعلَموا إنَّ الله مَعَ المُتقين
3. ...يَامُرهُم بِالمَعروفِ و يَنهاهُم عَن المُنكَرِ
4. و قاتِلوهُم فى سَبيل اللهِ الذين يُقاتِلونَكم ولاتَعتَدوا أن اللهَ لا يُحِب المُعتَدين
5. This verse is called the" verse of E'tedah"

When your enemy utilizes some strong or weak weapon, the opposite side must react proportionately, not utilize a very stronger weapon. But in retaliation against the nuclear weapon there is nothing for defending, and in case of retaliation the human generations will be jeopardized and will have many irreparable damages permanently.

b). The Principle of Distinction between Civilians and Combatants

The distinction between civilians and combatants includes: children, women, elderlies, patients, wounded, service powers, animals, trees, farms and generally environment. Based on this verse, the use of any weapon that is the instance of transgress is a major sin and forbidden in Islam. Likewise, the extension of war beyond the war zone that causes the harassment, even if for animals and environment is a major sin. Because it seems that the proscription in "E'tedah verse" is unconditional and includes any transgression, even about the environment.

1.2.1.1.2. Comments of the Qur'an Commentators

Fortunately, lots of Islamic commentators such as Sunnis and Shias, in addition to what was mentioned about the Islamic prohibition concerning the use of weapons of mass destruction, have very useful and great comments, some of which were mentioned:

1. Ayatollah Tabatabai believes that the prohibition of war extension beyond the war zone is unconditional and includes all children and elderlies (Tabatabai, 1955, p87) about the samples of "E'tedah verse" he expresses: if a war starts before the conciliation proposal, such war is religiously forbidden because it is the clear instance of the transgression.

2. Ayatollah Makaram states: based on the verse, in addition to the prohibition of war extension beyond the war zone, the

utilization of poisonous materials to pollute the enemies water sources, i.e. chemical and biological war is not permitted either. (Makarameshirazi, 1975, p9)

3. Moqaddase Ardabili believes: some samples of transgressions which have been specified under Islamic tenets consists of the beginning of war before the enemy, killing the atheist which is under the contract with Muslims and illegal killing (Moqaddaseardabili, p306).

The Sunni commentators, likewise the Shia commentators, have extracted the prohibition of WMD use from the E'tedah verse, for example:

4. Whba Zuhayli as a Sunni scholar in his exegesis (Almonir) states: the beginning of war, killing Muslims, war against civilians such as; children, elderlies, destruction of houses, tree felling and burning farms are the samples of transgression. (Zuhayli, 1997, p179)

1.2.1.2. Hadiths

1. Imam Ali (A.s) states: let your heart be replete with people kind and do not be like brutal animals toward them....because people are dividable into two groups; either are your religious brother or one like you in creation. (Sayyed Razi, 1994, p53)

2. The Hadiths from the holy Prophet and the other Imams have generality on Islamic prohibition of houses destruction, burning farms, killing civilians and animals, spreading toxins into the enemy's dwelling place. In this respect, Toosi narrates: When holy prophet had to have a war against enemies, he used to gather his soldiers and tell them: move in the name of God, in favor of his way and because of his religion, do not transgress, fulfill your obligations, do not kill children and elderlies, do not dismember and do not cut down trees unless it is inevitable. (Toosi, 1986,

p139)¹

Koleini as well narrates that: When Prophet chooses a commandant for war, always advises him to observing the divine piety toward himself and the other soldiers and then say fight in the name of God and in favor of God and only kill people who are atheist but fulfill your obligation and do not overdo and do not kill children and do not dismember. (Koleini, 1987, p30)²

There are some Hadiths that have been narrated by Sunni scholars, for instance Abi Shabih says: "in the name of God and based on the divine religion, free the captivates and do not kill children and women, do not indulge in order to increase your war spoils, be kind and do goodness because Allah loves them".(Abi Shabih, 1988, p654)³ Termezi also narrates that: "When Prophet chooses a commandant for war always advise him on observing the divine piety toward himself and the other soldiers and then say fight in the name of God and on behalf of God and only kill people who are atheist but fulfill your obligation and do not overdo and do not kill children and do not dismember"⁴"⁵. (Al Termezi, 1983, p86)

---

1. «محمد بن يعقوب عن على بن ابراهيم عن أبيه عن ابن إبى عمير عن معاوية بن عمار قال أظنه عن أبى حمزة‎ الثمالى عن أبى عبدالله ﷺ قال: كان رسول الله ﷺ اذا أراد أن يَبعث سرية دَعاهُم فأجلَسَهم بَين يديه ثُم يقول سيروا بِسم الله و بالله وفى سَبيل الله وعلى ملة رَسول الله ﷺ لا تغلوا ولاتمثلوا ولاتغدروا ولا تقتُلوا شيخاً فانياً ولا صَبياً ولاامرأةً ولا تَقطعوا شَجراً إلا أن تضطروا إليها...»

2. «عن على بن ابراهيم عن هارون بن مسلم عن مسعدة بن صدقة عن أبى عبدالله ﷺ قال: إن النبى ﷺ كان إذا أراد أن يَبعثَ أميراً على سرية أمَرَه بتقوى الله عزوجل فى خاصّة نفسِه ثُمَ فى اصحابه عامّة ثم يَقول أغزوا بسم الله وفى سَبيل الله قاتلوا مَن كَفر بالله ولا تغلوا ولا تَمثلوا ولاتَقتُلوا وليداً»

3. «عن خالد بن الفزر حدثنى أنس بن مالك أن رسول الله ﷺ قال: انطَلِقوا باسم الله ، وَبِاللهِ وَعَلى مِلَّةِ رَسُولِ اللهِ ، لا تَقتُلوا شَيخًا فَانِيًا ، وَلا طِفلا ، وَلا صَغيرًا ، وَلا امرَأةً ، وَلا تَغُلُوا ، وَضُمُّوا غَنائِمَكُم ، وَأَصلِحُوا وَأَحسِنُوا ، إنَّ اللهَ يُحِبُّ المُحسِنينَ النتهى»

4. Both scholars referred to the same quotation.

5. «عن سليمان بن بريدة عن أبيه قال كان رسول الله ﷺ إذا أمَّر أميراً على جيش أو سرّية أوصاه فى خاصّته بتقوى الله ومن معه من المُسلمينَ خيرٍ ائمَ قال اغزوا بِسم الله فى سبيل الله قَاتِلوا مَن كفر الله اغزوا ولا تغلوا ولا تغدروا ولا تمثُلوا ولاتقتُلوا وليداً. وإذا لقيتَ عدوّكَ من المشركين فادعُهم إلى إحدى ثلاثِ خصال.»

Each of the following principles which have been extracted from Quranic sources, can be argued for expressing the legal fundamentals of the use prohibition of unconventional nuclear and biological armaments:

I). prohibition of action battle with the intention of revenge and bleeding

II). prohibition of the beginning war before ultimatum and inviting to conciliation

III). prohibition of dismemberment of enemy's casualties

IV). prohibition of breach of war agreements and treaties

V). prohibition of cutting and burning trees and farms

VI). prohibition of captivating before ultimatum and inviting to conciliation

VII). prohibition of killing enemy's soldiers despite of the possibility of their captivation

VIII). prohibition of killing animals

IX). prohibition of war after accepting Islam by enemy

XI). prohibition of war against the Ahl al ketab[1] whereas they are ready for conciliation

XII). prohibition of extension of war after receiving the conciliation proposal by enemy

XIII). prohibition of houses and towns destruction

XIV). prohibition of water obstruction against the enemy

XV). prohibition of killing the escaping soldiers of enemy

XVI). prohibition of killing the civilians including: children, women, elderlies, monastics, nurses, wounded, patients and messengers

---

1. The followers of non-Islamic monotheistic religions.

XVII). prohibition of killing the enemy's soldiers which have participated in war by duress

XVIII). prohibition of killing the hirelings

XIX). prohibition of children participation in war

XX). prohibition of non-precision attacks in order to avoid unlawful damages

XXI). prohibition of disabled use in process of war

1.2.2. Study of the Conceptual Indications of Some Hadiths on Prohibition of Production and Usage of Nuclear Weapons

A). Some Nabavi[1] Hadiths in religious texts on prohibition of poisoning the enemy's dwelling; Holy Prophet has prohibited poisoning in polytheist's dwellings. (Toosi, 1986, p143)[2]

It seems that even though there is a prohibition on poisoning, it is not limited to poison and include all sorts of weapons of mass destruction, because there is no any difference among water, weather or land poisoning using the other unconventional weapons. Therefore, if there is the word of poison in Islamic texts, it refers to any weapon leading to the destruction of innocents out of war zones including, humans, animals, farms and environment. (Toosi, 1996, p143)

1.2.2.1. Some Supporting Implications:

Firstly: definitive priority, because when there is a prohibition on the usage of poison harming a limited area, usage of nuclear weapon is absolutely prohibited under Islam. Secondly: In wordings of Hadiths there is no any specific emphasis on water, weather or land, rather there is a general banning that includes all

---

1. Comes from holy Prophet.

2. «عن سكونى، عن جعفرعن ابيه عن على عليه السلام، ان النبّى صلى الله عليه وسلم نهى ان يلقى السّم فى بلاد المشركين»

sorts of WMD.

Thirdly: In such rules; that there is a prohibition because of a damaging nature, it is evident that the weapons of mass destruction, in terms of having the same function, definitely are forbidden. Fourthly: any extension of war to civilian areas is forbidden, no matter it happens by poison or any other kind of unconventional or nuclear weapons. Consequently; based on the indication of Hadiths on prohibition of poisoning in war and regarding the same function of WMD, it can be concluded, the use of nuclear weapon is religiously banned.

1.2.3. Comments of Islamic Scholars on the Prohibition of Poisoning During War

Based on these Hadiths, many scholars consider the poisoning on war and civilian areas unlawful, some of them include the followings:

1). Sheikheh-Toosi in his book (Al Nahayah) that in every legal case, expressing only the related Hadith, specifies the rule governing on the case by scrutinizing in "Hadith", instead of "argument", and expression of legal case - because the practice of Sheikh in this book is the issuance of the fatwa based on the wordings of Hadith- states: "indeed the poisoning on atheists dwelling is prohibited"[1]. (Toosi, 1979, p51)

2). Ibne Edris states: "killing the atheists is permitted, but that must be distinguished between fighters and civilians, also the use of poison is not acceptable, because poisoning in their dwelling is forbidden"[2]. (Helli, 1989, p7)

3). Abolmakarem believes that: "the poisoning in atheistic towns is prohibited, and fighting in forbidden months is unlawful, of course about some of those who believe in this rule, unless they start the

---

1. فانة لا يَجُوزُ أن يُلقَى فى بلادِهم السمَّ
2. يجوزُ قِتالُ الكُفارِ بسائرِ أنواعِ القتلِ واسبابِه الاّ بتَفريقِ الساكنِ وزميهِم بالغيرانِ والقاءِ سمٍ فى بلادِهم فانّه لا يَجوُز أن يُلقى السَمَ فى بلادِهم

war and Muslims have to be the defender".¹ (Abolmakarem, p201)

4). Karaki says: "if it is possible to be the winner without resorting to poisoning, use of poison in atheist realms is unlawful"². (Karaki, 1993, p385)

5). Shahid alavval believes that: "based on better comment, poisoning is prohibited"³. (Shahid alavval, 1996, p32)

6). Shahid Thani in his book (masalek) states: "poisoning for killing innocent people is forbidden"⁴. (Shahid Thani, 1992, p24)

7). Allamah Helli in his book (Ershad) States: "by various ways it is possible to fight against enemy but by resorting to poisoning, unless you have to do it"⁵. (Allamah Helli, 1990, p344)

8). Ayatollah Sadr, in addition to the fatwa on prohibition of poisoning the atheist dwellings, goes one step further and expresses: "even though in Sokoni's Hadith the title of poison has been utilized, but the poison undoubtedly does not have subjectivity, rather in terms of criterion includes any unconventional weapon". (Sadr, 1999, p384)

9). Grand Ayatollah Khoyi believes that: "based on Prophet's prohibition on poisoning the polytheists' realms, that is unlawful"⁶. (Khoyi, 1989, p371)

10). Lots of contemporary sources of emulation⁷ have prohibited in their fatwas the use of unconventional armaments during war. Ayatollah Makaram says: in addition to the prohibition of

---

1. فانه لا يَجُوزُ أن يُلقَى فى دِيارِهم القاء السَمّ ولا يُقاتل فى اشهر الحرام فى مَن يَرى لَها حرمَة من الكُفّار إلا أن يَبدأوا فيها بِالقِتالِ

2. «يحرُم القاء السمّ إن أمكَن الفتخ بدونه»

3. «ولا يجُوزُ القاء السَمّ على الأصَح»

4. «القاء السَمّ لوادى الى قتلِ نَفس مُحترمِه حرام لذالك»

5. «وتَجُوزُ المُحاربَة باصنافهم الا السَمّ ولو اضطَرّ اليه جَاز»

6. «لا يجُوز القاء السمّ فى بلاد المشركين لنهى النبى ﷺ فى معتبرَة السكّونى عن ابى عبدِالله عليه السلام قال قال امير المؤمنين ﷺ نَهى رسول الله ﷺ أن يُلقى السمّ فى بلادِ المُشركين»

7. The grand Islamic scholars that must be obeyed in Islamic rules by their imitators.

war extension to the civilian zones; elimination of jungle, farms and poisoning , i.e. chemical and biological war is forbidden. (Makaram, 1974, p9) According to the authentic Hadiths and previous and contemporary religious Scholars fatwa, the use of unconventional weapons is prohibited by religion, because it is recognized as the "modern sample" of poisoning.

B). Some Hadiths Indicate the Prohibition of Using the Incendiary Weapons during War

1). Based on this Hadiths, holy Prophet "bans the dates burning"[1]. (Al Ameli, 1988, p43)

2). Toosi narrates from holy Prophet; "do not punish by burning, because only God of fire has the right to punish by fire"[2]. (Toosi, 1986, p143)

1.2.4. Comments of Islamic Scholars on Incendiary Weapons

Many Scholars of the Islamic world, according to such Hadiths expressed: use of the incendiary weapons in the battle field is forbidden. Undoubtedly, part of the weapons of mass destruction is incendiary, hence they will be subject of these Fiqhi opinions. For example:

1). Mohagheghe Al Helli in Sharay'e believes that, any use of incendiary weapon is forbidden. (Mohaghegh, 1994, p66)

2). Mohaghegh Al Thani also illegalizes the use of incendiary weapons, burning the trees, agricultural crops, animals and the innocent. (Karaki, 1987, p385)

3). Ibne Al Edris is one of those who has expressed; "fighting by incendiary weapons is not permitted"[3]. (Helli, 1989, p7)

---

1. «عن ابى عبدالله ﷺ قال أن النبى ﷺ كان اذا بعث اميراً له على سرية امره بالتقوى الله عز وجل فى خاصة نفسه ثم فى اصحابه عامة ثم يقول اغز بسم اله وفى سبيل الله قاتلوا من كفر بالله ولا تغدروا ولا تغلوا و لا تمثلوا ولا تقتلوا وليداً ولا مبتلاً فى شاهق ولا تحرقوا النخل ولاتفرقوا بالماء ولا تقطعوا شجرة مثمر ولاتحرقوا زرعاً».

2. «عبدالله ابن مسعود عن ابيه قال رسول الله ﷺ لا تعذّبُوا بالنّار لا يعذّب بالنار اِلا رَبها».

3. «يجوز قتال الكفار... الا رميهم بالنيران».

Conclusion: According to the valid Hadiths and fatwas, it can be concluded that, any use of unconventional armaments during a war is prohibited, because they can be recognized as the samples of incendiary weapons.

1.2.5. Islamic Scholars View about the Banning the Use of WMD

1.2.5.1. Shia Scholars

The Shia Scholars, based on the E'tedah verse and other valid Hadiths, believe that the use of weapons leading to mass destruction is prohibited and the principle of distinction and proportionality must be considered, nevertheless, WMD absolutely cannot cover such principles and lead to irreparable damages for nature and humanity. Some of them include the followings:

1). Do not let the polytheist wives help them in war against Muslims, but in case of coerce you can kill them[1]. (Toosi, 1979, p292)

2). When there is no any necessity, you do not have right to kill women during war[2]. (Alborraj, 1985, p303)

3). In war against polytheists, when one of them obeyed you and accepted your logic, his killing is not permitted because he is your religious brother. If he is unruly, try to control him and if they are not combatant, their killing is not permitted[3]. (Helli, 1912, p911)

---

1. «ولا يَجوزُ قتالُ النساءِ. فإن قاتَلَنَ المسلمينَ وعاونَ أزواجَهنَّ ورجالَهنَّ، أمسِك عنهنَّ. فإن اضطُرّوا إلى قتلِهنَّ، جازَ حينئذٍ قتلُهنّ، ولم يكُن بَه بأسٌ»

2. «ولايَجوزُ قتلُ النساءِ وإن قَتلنَ مع أهلِهنَّ، إلا أن يَدعو إلى قتلِهنَ ضرورةٌ، وإن دَعت ذلك ضرورةٌ لم يَكن به بأسٌ»

3. «لا يجوز قتل صبيان المشركين إجماعاً ولا نسائهم والمجانين منهم روي الجمهور عن يونس بن مالك أن النبي ﷺ قال: انطلقوا باسم الله وبالله وعلى ملة رسول الله ﷺ لا تقتلوا شيخاً كبيراً فانياً ولا صغيراً و لا امرأةً ومن طريق الخاصة ما رواه الشيخ في الحسن عن أبي حمزة الثمالي عن أبي عبدالله ﷺ قال: كان رسول الله ﷺ إذا أراد أن يبعث سرية رعاهم فأجلسهم بين يديه ثم يقول لهم سيروا باسم الله و بالله وفي سبيل الله وعلى ملة رسول الله ﷺ الا تعلوا ولا تمثلوا ولا تغدروا ولا تقتلوا شيخاً فانياً ولا صبياً ولا امرأة و أيما رجل من أدنى المسلمين وأفضلهم نظر إلى أحد من المشركين فهو جار حتى أن يسمع كلام الهفان تبعكم فأخوكم في دينكم وإن بغت فاستعينوا بالله عليه و أبلغوا به

4). During war; killing the insane, children and women of polytheists is not permitted unless there is a necessity[1]. (Helli, 1992, p486)

5). Only in case of necessity, killing the insane, children and women in war against polytheists is permitted[2]. (Helli, 2000, p80)

6). Do not kill elderlies, children and women[3]. (Najafi, p73)

7). Holy Prophet has banned killing the children, elderlies and disabled in war against polytheists and atheists[4]. (Miyanji, 1990, p91)

1.2.5.2. Sunni Scholars

The Sunni Scholars, like the Shia Scholars, based on the Verses and Hadiths have issued the Fatwas on prohibition of WMD and any action leading to the extension of war to civilian zones and destruction of houses, trees, farms, animals and environment, here I mention some of them

1.2.5.2.2. Hanafi Scholars:

1). in war against enemies of religion; insane, women, child, blind, cripple, hand-cut and disable elderlies must not be killed[5]. (Al Hanafi, 1998, p128)

2). the basis of war against someone is his ability in fighting, hence

---

مأمنه. ولأنهم ليسوا من أهل المحاربة فلا ينبغي قتلهم»

1. «لا يَجوزُ قتلُ المَجانينِ، ولا الصِّبيانِ، ولا النِّساءِ مِنهُم و إن أعنَّ إلا مَعَ الحَاجَةِ»

2. «ولا يَجوزُ قتلُ المَجانينِ و الصبيانِ و النساءِ و إن أعنَّ، ولَو تترسوا كفَّ عنهم إلا مَعَ الضرورة»

3. «ولا يجوز قتل المجانين ولا الصبيان ولا النساء منهم ولو عاونوهم بتشديد النون إلا مع الاضطرار بلا خلاف اجده فى شىء من ذلك، بل فى المنتهى الإجماع عليه فى النساء و الصبيان، بل وَعَلَى قتل النساء مع الضرورة، مضافا إلى ماسمعته من خبرى جَميلِ والشمالى و غير هُما، بل فى رواية الجمهور عن أنس بن مالك أن النبى ﷺ قال: «انطلقوا بسم اللهِ و بالله و على ملة رسول الله ﷺ و لا تقتلوا شيخاً فانياً ولا صغيراً ولا امرأة»

4. «نهى رسول الله ﷺ عن قتل مَن لا يُقاتل فى مَكة، و نَهى عن قَتل النساء والصبيان والشيوخ الذين لا يُقاتلون ولا يعينون المقاتلين ولو بالتدبير والفكر. كما نهى عن قتل العُسفاء والوَصفاء والرهبان والمقعد وأصحاب الصوامع الذين لا تدخل لهم فى حزب المسلمين بأى نحو و إليك النصوص»

5. «ولا يَقتلوا مَجنوناً، ولا امرأةً ولا صَبياً، ولا أعمى، ولا مَقعداً، ولا مَقطوع اليمين، ولا شيخاً فانياً»

the aforementioned people do not include this basis[1]. (Al Shokani, 2001, p411)

3). The elderlies, children, disables, women and civilians must not be damaged during war against enemy[2]. (Al Enayah, p425)

4). When Allah has said raise against people who have raised against you, we can conclude that there is no any permission for war against the disabled, because they cannot raise against anybody[3]. (Sarakhsi, 1996, p450)

1.2.5.2.3. Shafe'i Scholars

1). Because of Nabavi[4] prohibition, Muslims do not have the right to kill disabled and women, also killing the intersexes is not permissible, because in case of doubt about the gender of person, Muslims must treat with caution and let them be live[5]. (Al Noovi, p295)

2). Shafei said: Holy Prophet has prohibited his soldiers from killing women and children[6]. (Ibne Edris, 1983, p253)

3). Killing children, women, the insane and intersexes has been

---

1. «ولا يقتُلُوا امراة ولا صَبياً و لا شَيخاً فانياً ولا مَقعداً ولا أعمَى لأن المُبيح للقَتَل عندنا هو الحِراب ولا يَتَحقَّقُ، منهُم، ولهذا لا يَقتل يابسِ الشَقِ والمقطوع اليمنى والمقطوع يده ورجلهِ من خلافٍ»

2. « ولا يقتُلُوا امراة ولا صَبياً و لا شَيخاً فانياً ولا مَقعداً ولا أعمَى لأنالمُبيح للقتل عندنا هو الحِراب ولا يتحَقَّقُ منهم». ولهذا لا يَقتل يابسِ الشَقِ والمقطوع اليمنى والمقطوع يده ورجلهِ من خلافٍ»

3. «لا ينبغي أن يقتل النساء من أهل الحرب ولا الصبيان ولا المجانين ولا الشيخ الفاني، لقوله تعالى "وقاتلوا في سبيل الله الذين يقاتلوكم" وهؤلاء لا يقاتلون وحين استعظم رسول الله ﷺ و قتل النساء أشار إلي هذه بقوله: هاه، ماكانت هذه تقاتل أدرك خالداً وقل له: لا تقتلن ذرية ولا عسيفاً»

4. Stated by Holy Prophet.

5. « (فصل) ولا يجوز قتل نسائهم ولا صيانهم إذا لم يقاتلوا لما روي ابن عمر رضي الله عنه أن رسول الله ﷺ نهي عن قتل النساء و الصبيان ولا يجوز قتل الخنثي المشكل، لانه يجوز أن يكون رجلاً ويجوز أن يكون امرأة فلم يقتل مع الشك»

6. «(قال الشافعى) رحمه الله تعالى ولا يَجوز لاحدٍ من المسلمينَ أن يَعمد قتلَ النساء و الوالدان لان رسولَ الله ﷺ نهي عن قتلهم أخبرنا سفيان عن الزهري عن ابن كعب ابن مالك عن عمه أن رسول الله ﷺ نهى الذين بعثَ إلى ابن أبى الحقيقِ عن قتلَ النساء والولدان»

prohibited[1]. (Al Sherbini, 1958, p223)

4). Majority of Scholars have expressed, if women and children raised against the Muslims in order to kill them, in this case killing them is permitted[2]. (Al Noovi, 1999, p48)

1.2.5.2.4. Hanbali Scholars

1). Ibne Abbas in his comment on the verse 190 of Baqarah[3] has said: killing women and children and elderlies is prohibited[4]. (Ghodamah, p544)

2). Under the Islamic jurisprudence, not killing atheist women and children after Muslims domination is a well-stablished rule, especially when there is a Nabavi Hadiths in this respect.[5] (Al Abdoalrahman, p400)

1.2.5.2.5. Maliki Scholars

1). There is an authentic Hadiths from holy Prophet proscribing killing women and children, accordingly that is forbidden under Islam[6]. (Alazhari, p414)

2). Based on Quran and Sunnah[7], killing children, women, elderlies

---

1. «ویحرُم علیه قتل صَبی ومجنونِ و امره و خنثی مشکل. الشرح: (ویحرم علیه قتل صبی و مجنون) و من به رق (وامراة و خنثی مشکل) للنهی عن قتل الصبیان و النساء فی الصَحیحینف والخَق المجنون بالصبی، والخنثی بالمراة لاحتمال أنوثته»

2. «قوله (نهی رسول الله ﷺ عن قتل النساء و الصبیان) أجمَعَ العلماءُ علی العمل بهذا الحدیثِ و تحریم قتلِ النساءِ والصبیانِ إذا لم یقاتِلوا فأن قاتلوا قال جماهیر العلماءِ یَقتلون»

3. One of the Quranic Suras (chapter).

4. « ولا تقتل امرأة ولا شیخ فإن وبذلک قال مالک و أصحاب الرأی، وروی ذلک عن أبی بکر الصدیق ومجاهد. وروی عن ابن عباس فی قوله تعالی (ولاتعتدوا) یقول لا تقتلوا النساء الصبیان والشیخ الکبیر»

5. « (وإذا ظفربهم لم یقتل صبی ولاامراة ولا شیخ فإن ولا أعمی، ولا راهب ولا رأی لهم الا ان یقاتلوا) إذا ظفر بالکفار لم یجز قتل صبی لم یبلغ بغیر خلاف لما روی ابن عمر رضی الله عنهما ان النبی ﷺ نهی عن قتل النساء و الصبیان، متفق علیه ولان الصبی یصیر رقیقاً بنفس السبی ففی قتله إتلاف المال و إذا سبی منفرداً صار مسلماً فاتلافه اتلاف من یمکن جعله مسلماً»

6. «ولا یقتل النساء و لا الصبیان لما صح من نهیه علیه الصلاة والسلام عن قتلهم»

7. Lifestyle of Holy Prophet.

and hirelings has been banned[1]. (Al Gharafi, 1994, p389)

As highlighted above, the nuclear fatwa has very deep Quranic and Revayi[2] roots, insofar as any probability of its reversibility is impossible. After the investigating on religious fundamentals of the nuclear fatwa, the other aspect of fatwa must be analyzed, which includes its governmental status; because this fatwa has been issued by the competent Mujtahid that is recognized as the leader of Muslims and his decree according to Iran's Constitution is binding for triple powers[3] which includes all parts of State and as well all people. As this decree is primary, therefore will be permanently irreversible. No necessity has this potential to change this decree.

1.3. Governmental Decree under Islamic Tenets

There are some differences and similarities among the primary and secondary governmental decree and institution of fatwa under Islamic tenets and that is why some researchers make a mistake in correct evaluation of the exact format of nuclear fatwa and subsequently determination of its religious status. Therefore, some concepts and terms must be defined and explained here.

1.3.1. Relationships between Fatwa and Governmental Decree

Fatwa: is the expression of divine ruling about something by Faqih with regarding to (Quran, Prophet Traditions, Consensus and Reason). Fatwa has "declarative" aspect, in which Faqih just declare the divine rules about related cases. Differently, governmental decree has innovative aspect and is the order of

---

1. «وها هنا تفريعان الأول فى الكتاب لا يقتل النساء ولا الصبيان ولا المشايخ الكبار ولا الرهبان فى الصوامع و الديارات ويترك لهم من أموالهم ما يعيشون به و نهى عن قتل العسيف وهوالأجير و فى مسلم نهى عن قتال النساء والصبيان وفى النسائى لاتقتلوا ذرية ولا عسيفاً»

2. Based on lots of Hadiths.
3. Executive, legislative and judiciary.

Islamic leader emanating from Islamic sources about related cases. Furthermore, obedience domain of fatwa is limited to the emulators of the sources of emulation[1], whereas compliance with a governmental decree is necessary for all including the sources of emulation and their emulators one by one.

Primary Governmental Decree: is Islamic leader's edict which is in line with divine rules completely, in a way that enjoys the declarative aspect as well. Its issuance is only a kind of emphasis on what has been already determined by God, not a new rule. On contrary, Secondary governmental decree is not necessarily in line with primary Islamic rules, in this case the durability of such decree will be limited to existence of an expediency. However, some Islamic experts believe that the primary and secondary rules are different from governmental decree in kind.

Nuclear fatwa in the sense that has been issued by the Islamic governor is a governmental decree, in the sense that has been issued by one of the sources of emulation is fatwa and from this point that is identically the indication of divine rule in a declarative not innovative way; is primary not secondary. For example, what was issued by Ayatollah Khomeini in prohibition of Hajj had the innovative aspect, subsequently was a secondary governmental decree. The other fact which guarantees the primality of nuclear fatwa is about its performance time. Secondary governmental decree is performed just for a short time, for example, The "Tobacco" decree was performed just for some months or Ayatollah Khomeini's decree in prohibition of Hajj; whereas nuclear fatwa, will be performed forever undoubtedly, because only reflects the unchangeable Islamic fundamentals.

The subject of a governmental decree may be different functionally. In some cases, decree proscribes something that is

---

1. Islamic high level experts that people must obey them in performance of the Islamic rulings.

indispensable religiously, in this case decree seems to be against the Islamic jurisprudence, whereas in a higher horizon, is in line with Islamic tenets like decree of Hajj by Imam Khomeini. Sometimes that is about the permissible acts like the decree of Tobacco. But in some other cases, that is also possible that a decree proscribe something which has been proscribed before like nuclear fatwa, in such a case there is a primary prohibition against related subject and issuance of fatwa is only a kind of emphasis in that regard and reflection of previous fundamental principles as well.

1.3.2. Authenticity Reasons of Governmental Decree

A). Quran:

Part: Nisa, verse 59: "O you who believe! Obey Allah and obey the Messenger (Muhammad), and those of you (Muslims) who are in authority. (And) if you differ in anything amongst yourselves, refer it to Allah and His Messenger, if you believe in Allah and in the resurrection. That is better and more suitable for final determination."[1]

There is no any doubt that this verse indicates the validity of governmental decrees. In fact, obedience is not realized, unless by complying with decrees. In this verse, obedience of three sources has been listed, first God, second Prophet Muhammad and third some Muslims in authority. Just the third part relates to our discussion as the validity of the Islamic governor's decrees. The view of Islamic scholars about the exact meaning of "… Muslims in authority…" are divided into three main groups, two of which are special and one is general.   Generally, the majority of Islamic scholars believe that the purpose of the verse contains Mujtahids and Faqihs (Ardabili, 1996, p861). The special groups of Sunnis believe that it includes all authorities, even if be cruel (Al

---

1. يَا أَيُّهَا الَّذِينَ آمَنُوا أَطِيعُوا اللهَ وَأَطِيعُوا الرَّسُولَ وَأُولِي الْأَمْرِ مِنكُمْ فَإِن تَنَازَعْتُمْ فِي شَيْءٍ فَرُدُّوهُ إِلَى اللهِ وَالرَّسُولِ إِن كُنتُمْ تُؤْمِنُونَ بِاللهِ وَالْيَوْمِ الْآخِرِ ذَلِكَ خَيْرٌ وَأَحْسَنُ تَأْوِيلًا

Sayes, 1994, p482). Shia scholars believe that the purpose of the verse is the best people who are only Imams and in their absence, the highest ranks of Faqihs in all aspects (Tabatabai, 1999, p139).

B). Traditions:

There are many Prophetic and Imami[1] quotations and narrations which refer to the incumbency of implying with Faqihs decrees, including Ibne-Hanzaleh (Ameli, p136). According to this narration, Imam Sadeq has proscribed Muslims from obeying cruel governors, and has appointed Faqihs as the governors for Muslims.

C). Reason:

There is no any doubt that even if we fail to bring the Traditional reasons to support the authenticity of governmental decrees, rational reasons, as one of the fourfold sources, can be mentioned. The Reason which, in narrations, has been considered as the intrinsic messenger (Koleini, p16) and Imam Sadeq imparted:" Whoever is wise, is religious as well and will enter heaven (Koleini, p11)." Reason based on some conditions, perceive the necessity of the system formation as a government and sovereignty in order to avoid anarchism in society and, subsequently, confirms the importance of governmental decrees and their role in realization of order and organization. Hence, some Islamic scholars try to prove the authenticity of such decrees just by rational arguments (Naraghi, 1996, p518).

1.3.3. Thematic Domain of Governmental Decree

Is the decree subject only limited to the religious aspects or not it can also include some other aspects beyond that?

In response to the question, it must be said that if the duty

---

1. From Imams.

of Islamic ruler is only running of religious rulings, and not the management of the secular affairs of society, he is not entitled to issue decrees in the scope of secular affairs. But based on the religious texts and noted scholar works it's evident that the authority of the Islamic ruler is not limited to the religious aspects of people's social life; to sum up, his task is the "maintenance of both people's religion and world".

1.3.4. Temporal Domain of Governmental Decree

How long is a governmental decree valid?

In this regard some assumptions are supposable:

1. Governmental decrees, bounded by a specific time; obviously, when the life of a governmental decree is bounded by a specific time, after elapsing the due date, will be invalidated.

2. Governmental decrees, concerning some special subjects; if a governmental decree is issued based on a subject which no longer exists, the governmental decree is automatically terminated too. Like some special rules derived from a governmental decree concerning the war time, evidently, after the termination of war, such rules will not be binding.

3. Governmental decrees limited to a necessity; similar to what mentioned about the first assumption, sometimes issuance of a governmental decree emanates from a necessity, naturally, the survival of governmental decree will last as long as the necessity (Javadiyeamoli, 1998, p138).

1.4. *Governmental Decree[1] in the Iranian Constitution*

1.4.1. Constitution and the Issuance Authority of Governmental Decree by the Supreme Leader

---

1. This is a legal translation for phrase the of "*Hokme Hokoomaty* "regardless of being primary or secondary.

After a brief introduction of Islamic approaches in connection with weapons of mass destruction and investigation of unchangeable fundamentals of the Nuclear Fatwa, now, under the legal system of Islamic Republic of Iran, that is very valuable to be analyzed, what is the domestic legal status of a governmental decree as an aspect of the Nuclear Fatwa? And also, is it possible to legalize the authority of the supreme leader in the issuance of such orders by citation from the Constitution? It's obvious that our assumption in this debate is the legitimacy and authenticity of the issued decrees by the supreme leader and what comes after this is the depiction of this legal basis. In this part of the research, first the general axes relating to the position of governmental decrees and the leader's authority in the issuance of these decrees are discussed, and then considered some related principles (articles) in Constitution.

1.4.1.1. General Axes

1.4.1.2. Islamic Nature of System and Governmental Decree

In a general view, it can be stated that the principle axis and base of Iran's political system and Constitution is «Islamic rules and Jurisprudence». Iranian nation basically raised against the monarch regime, with the purpose of realizing the Islamic system and as well operationalization of Islamic rules, under the guidance of the religious leadership. On this basis, the first step of the nation, after the Islamic revolution, was the establishment of Islamic Republic of Iran, and then the ratification of Constitution based on Islamic rules. Thus, the various evidences and signs of the Islamic superiority throughout the Constitution is evident. For example, Islamic nature of the system (principle one), dependency of the system on faith bases (including: principles of religion and Sharia, principle two), the non-diversion of rules and regulations from the Islamic sacred jurisprudence (principle four), the acceptance of the principle of Vilayateh Faqih in the absence of Imam Mahdi (principle five & fifty seven), institutionalization of the religious institutes, such as Consultation (principle seven) and "ordinance to virtue and the interdiction of vice" (principle eight), the conditionality of enjoyment from a great number of citizen rights, based on compliance with Islamic rules and tenets (principles nineteen to forty). These cases, and some other same ones, indicate that the governing spirit on Constitution and the will of lawmakers, imply the necessity of Islamic rules and jurisprudence enforcement in all political, economic, cultural, and social dimensions. Therefore, the Islamic nature of system or the centrality of Islam and its rules in Iran's political system and Constitution, itself, is an evidence for the principle position of the governmental decree of Valiyeh Faqih (supreme leader). With this expression that Islamic rules, in addition to the inclusion of the primary and secondary rules, also include the administrative rules that are issued by Valiyeh Faqih which are emanated from Islamic jurisprudence. Thus the sine qua non for the acceptance of the Islamic rules sovereignty and Islamic political system, is the acceptance of the validity of such decrees and the issuance possibility of governmental decrees by Valiyeh Faqih.

1.4.1.3. Vilayateh Faqih and Governmental Decree

As a momentous governmental entity in Constitution (principle five& fifty seven), the institutionalization of the Velayateh Faqih principle is one of the most significant achievements of the Islamic revolution. Vilayateh Faqih that is rooted in the religious fundamentals and has adopted its legitimacy from divine rules, means that, the competent Valiyeh Faqih, in dealing with national affairs, has the authority as much as holy Prophet and infallible Imams (Imam Khomeini, 1956, p75-102). It means that, as those eminences had the authority to issue governmental decrees, also

Valiyeh Faqih, for to managing country, has right to issue such decrees. That is evident that as the issuance of such edicts have been based on Islamic principles (Ibid, p112-113) Valiyeh Faqih also must obey this procedure in issuance of governmental decrees. Consequently, Islamic nature of system and acceptance of Islamic rules and jurisprudence on one hand, and institutionalization of the Vilayateh Faqih principle on the other, per se, signify the issuance possibility of governmental decrees- which under the statute law has been considered as "rules and regulation with legal commitment"- by Valiyeh Faqih as a legal constitution.

1.4.2. Some Constitutional Evidence for Authority and Authenticity of Leader's Governmental Decree.

In addition to the two abovementioned references to Constitution, some other principles of this source indicate the right and authority of Valiyeh Faqih to issue such decrees, such as:

1.4.2.1. Article (Principle)[1] Hundred Ten:

Even though all parts of this principle per se are examples of governmental decree which is issued by Valiyeh Faqih, but some provisions of this principle directly signify the authority of supreme leader to issue these edicts, including:

Part One:

Based on this part, one of the obligations of the leader is "The determination of system's general policies, after consulting with expediency discernment council of the system". Hitherto, supreme leadership, has confirmed and imparted various policies in several executive fields of State, after the ratification and suggestion of the expediency discernment council of system, in order to run this part. Our purpose from policies, are the "policies that in order to realization of aims and values are put after the set

---

1. In Iranian Constitutional law articles of Constitution are called principle.

of ideals and include the principles which approximate the ideals to the executive concepts that are operationalized within system containing the triple powers, armed forces, national broadcasting, and the powers that are active within the society which includes (general, sectional and ultra-sectional) policies".

Reconsideration of the definition and characteristics of governmental decree, introduces the general policies of system as the most obvious examples of such edicts. The important trait of these policies is their superiority over all rules and regulations, i.e. the ratification and impartation of these policies by the leader, firstly; lead to revocation of adverse previous rules, and also the next rules and regulations must be ratified based on these decrees. Secondly, all powers and executive tools must implement these policies.

Part Seven:

One of the other obligations of the leader in the seventh part of principle 110 has been specified: "settlement of disputes and harmonization of relations among the triple powers". Disputes here means, sometimes because of non-liquet, vagueness or conflict of rules, some problems appear in relations among the triple powers and no regulation, in order to solve such disputes, has been predicted. In this case based on the pertinences of the leadership position, he takes action to solve the problem. It is completely obvious that what leader does in this respect is recognizable only under the title of governmental decrees and whereby, all State powers must comply with it. In other words, when the harmonization of relations among the triple powers, and the settlement of their disputes by the leader can be possible that leadership enjoys such authorities and others have to be obeyed by him. This general obedience, under the Islamic literature, is called "Hokmeh Hokoomati", or what we call governmental decree. Otherwise, basically such jurisdiction and authority will not be applicable by leader.

Part Eight:

In part eight of principle 110, "solving the problems of system - which are not solvable through usual methods- through the Expediency Discernment Council of the System" set forth as one of the obligations of supreme leader. According to the statements of the Revision Council of Constitution members, the "problems of system" relate to country management in a way that are not solvable by usual ways including lawmaking. It is evident that supreme leader, based on the authority that has been received from this part, can solve the problems of system through the expediency discernment council of system. Accordingly, what supreme leader issues in this respect, has the aspect of governmental decree which has been issued with the consultation of the expediency council and is consequently indispensable.

According to some researchers, the content of part 7 and 8 of principle 110, signify Vilayateh Faqih as well (Javadiyehamoli, 2004, p479). Hence, regardless of what mentioned, it can be concluded that these two parts per se signify the issuance possibility of governmental decrees by Valiyeh Faqih.

1.4.2.2. Article Hundred Twelve

The revision council of Constitution, by the codification of this principle, more than any other thing, has spoken about governmental decree. In this principle the expediency discernment council of system has been institutionalized. The record of this principle related to Imam Khomeini's letter in response to heads of powers about "How the Islamic ruler's rights, in case of governmental decrees, are applied" (Khomeini, 1965, p464). In the letter text whereby a governmental decree, he founded the expediency council. With regard to this record, the perception of the revision council members from Imam Khomeini's letter was this fact that the axis of this letter and formation basis of the expediency council is the" governmental decrees of supreme leader". On this basis, the first duty of the expediency council was predicted: " the discernment of system expediency by governmental decrees of the leader, in case of disagreement between the Guardian council and Parliament, after the passage of legal steps (Negotiations for the revision of Constitution, sessions 15-28, p 835&1522). The unequivocal remarks of the aforementioned council members, confirmed the fact that, basically the philosophy of the expediency council formation is the application of this task which had been stipulated in the part one of the suggested principle. However, due to the clearness of the " governmental decree" centrality in tasks of the expediency council, some members of the revision council, based on this fact that the disagreements between the guardian council and parliament is not always about the governmental decrees, considered the phrase of governmental decree unnecessary in text of principle 112 and subsequently suggested its elimination. Even though this suggestion could not be directly ratified, but finally after the long negotiations, the aforementioned principle was ratified, whereas the phrase of governmental decrees had been eliminated.

Anyway, based on what mentioned, that was clarified that basically the axis and basis of the principle 112 and formation of expediency council was the "explanation of the executive way of applying the Islamic ruler right in governmental decree cases" and "explanation of governmental decree" as well. This is the other evidence for acceptance of governmental decree of leader under Iranian Constitution.

1.4.2.3. The Other Articles of Constitution

Heretofore, we discussed some cases that were more important than the others, but in addition to the aforementioned cases, we can cite some other principles of Constitution in order to consolidate the status of governmental decree under the Constitution, these principles relate to the ultimate authority of leadership in the political pyramid, and the structure of the State including, principles fifty seven, sixty, hundred thirteen. All these principles indicate the superiority of leader's legal status on the other State powers. This status deserves to issue some appropriate orders in case of an expediency or necessity, and the other power and authorities must obey them. Accepting this fact, means accepting the possibility of the issuance of governmental decree by Valiyeh Faqih (supreme leader). At the end of this part of discussion, it must be stated that, in addition to principles of Constitution on authenticity of governmental decrees, there are some other sources of Constitutional law that can be cited. These sources include: the custom of leadership, wills of Imam Khomeini, statute rules and etc.

1.4.3. Legal Status of Governmental Decree under the Constitutional law of Islamic Republic of Iran

After talking over the position of governmental decree under the Constitution, in this part we pay attention to the importance and position of these edicts under the Constitutional law of Islamic Republic of Iran.

1.4.3.1. Governmental Decree of Valiyeh Faqih as One of the Sources of Constitutional law

"In talking over the sources of law, the main purpose, is an access to the kind of sources which interfere with genesis and formation of the rules of law" (Katozian, 2006, p5). The most important source of Constitutional law in every country is its Constitution. The other sources of Constitutional law in Iran include: the custom of leaders, judicial practice, doctrine, the regulation of parliament and etc. Some researchers, in addition to the principle sources of Constitutional law, consider the "works of politicians" and even their memories and biographies as the subsidiary sources of Constitutional law. (Qazi, 1993, p 117)

In addition to the customary sources of law, with regard to this fact that Iran's legal system is based on Islamic jurisprudence, the "Islamic source and rules" is considered as one of the sources of law generally and one of the sources of Constitutional law specifically. In Iran's legal system, one of the sources of Constitutional law is "governmental decree" which, on one hand, is rooted in Islamic jurisprudence and whereby gets the legitimacy, and on the other, is recognized as the noted sample of the politician works. The authority of governmental decree means that the rules of Constitutional law can be extracted by them and whereby edicts can be issued. That is evident that these legal rules have generality and in the same cases, are applicable.

The most evident examples of such decrees, which have made some rules, are the general policies of system that are applicable in several fields as the authentic legal rules. The governmental decree of Imam Khomeini about the foundation of Special Court of Clergy (1979), formation of the Supreme Council of Cultural Revolution (1980), and the legalization of its regulations (1984) and the governmental decree of Ayatollah Khamenei about the impartation of the law of courts and Special Court of Clergy as well (1990) are the other examples.

1.4.3.2. Governmental Decree of Valiyeh Faqih, the Extraordinary Situations and Crisis

Part three of principle hundred nine, has prescribed some specific managerial abilities for supreme leader as a necessity. According to this part, supreme leader must enjoy the "correct political and social insight, foresight, courage, management, and enough power for leadership". The important effect of these abilities are the capability of supreme leader in dealing with difficult situations related to the task of leader in running affairs. Possessing such abilities, Valiye Faqih appears in the political scene as a powerful and proficient manager. The power, management and sovereignty of every ruler in society depend on his great foresight, decision-making, and managing extraordinary situations. Some political researchers believe that a ruler is a person who makes a decision in crisis.

The exceptional situation includes any kind of riot and political or economic unrests which its control requires utilizing some extraordinary mechanisms. In these situations, the law-based order is not practical, rather there is a severe need to authority of the ruler. According to western politicians, the rulers of liberal sovereignty that is based on man-made statute law cannot overcome such situations, because they can only take steps in a determined way of rules, whereas in such situations, the rate of the legal jurisdiction must be unlimited. (Smith, 2011)

Differently, according to the fundamentals of Islamic sovereignty, the leader of Islamic Community can take action based on knowledge and justice -two features that are *sine qua non* for leadership (Imam Khomeini, 1955, p68) - and without confrontation with legal impasses. The tool at the Islamic leader's disposal is "governmental decree".

The supreme leader, in a commentary on Vilayateh Faqih, introduced it in meaning of "flexibility". It means that the institution of Vilayat must be able to regularly alter himself based on social transformations -that are part of human life customs-. In other words, when there is a flexibility at the main decision-maker of system disposal can whereby correct and alter the way of society. For example, about the foundation of Islamic banking, this method was used. The main idea in this commentary on

Vilayateh Faqih, is seeking a remedy in order to refrain from confrontation with straits and impasses. The key tool to refrain from such straits at the leader's disposal is "governmental decree". Therefore, Vilayateh Faqih can, in extraordinary and exceptional cases, in order to avoid such straits, save the system from challenge and crises through the issuance of governmental decrees. This expression is the other reading from the "settlement of disputes among the triple powers" (part7, principle110) and "solving the problems of system" (part8, principle110) that was mentioned before. The annals of Islamic revolution has repeatedly experienced the issuance of various governmental decrees -with this function- by Imam Khomeini and Ayatollah Khamenei.

The other kind of exceptional situation is "crisis". Some majors like management and sociology deal with the concept of crisis and its solutions. In short, "crises are events which happen quickly and, because of their epidemic nature, develop in a short time and affect several political, social, decision making fields. They must be controlled, otherwise several parts of a political system are affected in a way that its daily activities are destructed, and impose a critical situation on their function. With regard to this fact that the emergence of such a situation is along with costs and negative social and political consequences, and the danger of its continuation will impose some irreparable damages on the legitimacy of political system, the foresight of crisis and planning in order to control it, is the task of a decision-making unit in the framework of "crisis management".

Crisis management, is the logical process of confrontation with crisis insofar as: 1. it leads to its control and restitution 2. Preserves the fundamental values and interests which, in result of crisis, have been threatened. In some texts, crisis management has been considered as a kind of strategic tact in which the intrinsic and extrinsic layers of a crisis are analyzed, and whereby the necessary recognition is gained to creation of related tactics and guidance of elites towards problem-solving. (Tajik, 2000, p83) In Islamic Republic of Iran, the decision-making unit is "leader or Valiyeh Faqih", in this way that the leader, as the highest authority of country (principle113), the superior power on the triple powers (principle57) and as a person who enjoys enough knowledge (part1 of principle110), necessary justice and virtue (part2 of principle110), social and political insight and the skills of tact and management for leadership (part3 of principle110), is the most competent post to save the country in case of crisis.

Obviously, the leader's tool in this regard is "governmental decree" which is binding for all and is considered as the last State ultimatum. This is one of the distinctive privileges of Islamic system compared to other political systems that in case of confrontation with crisis do not have such a practical tool. The annals of Islamic Revolution has always experienced a great many crises which have been frustrated by supreme leader's governmental decrees. Some of these crises, with a severity actually much less than what has been occurred in Iran, led to the destruction of many countries.

Accordingly, and with regard to issuance of the nuclear Fatwa by supreme leader indicating Iran's general policy in connection with nuclear activities, the performance bond of this edict is the set forth principles of Constitution that make any violation of governmental decrees impossible. A clear related example is the governmental decree of supreme leader on the Intelligence Minister reinstatement; after he stepped down by the time president, Supreme leader lawfully reinstated him, subsequently Dr. Ahmadinejad, in a letter addressed the leadership, referring to principle 57 of Constitution, declared that the operationalization of the aforementioned "governmental decree" will be definitive and irreversible. On the other side, if the decree aspect of this Fatwa is not recognized, will not have any authenticity under international law, because a Fatwa does not only relate to international law and merely is respectable for imitators of a Mujtahed[1]. Therefore, what is authentic under international law is the formal statements of officials. Based on our assumption, even though this statement has been issued in a religious decree form, however is a binding manifestation by the major figure of state that will be talked more about it in the next chapters.[2]

---

1. The person who is considered as a religious authority and must be imitated in religious rules.

2. According to Iranian Constitutuion, ousting ministers is part of a Presidential authority unless it is rejected by Leadership. Since Dr, Ahmadinejad found Supreme leader letter in Status of a governmental decree re-invited Mr. Moslehi to cabinet.

Chapter Two

Authenticity of Nuclear Fatwa in Law Case of International Court of Justice and 2006 Act of International law Commission concerning the Unilateral Acts of States

In this chapter the authenticity of the nuclear fatwa from the perspective of the international law will be analyzed, and through it we inevitably study the law of evidence before international courts, the nature of a unilateral declaration, its authenticity, and finally its comparative study with nuclear fatwa. Accordingly, the authenticity of the nuclear fatwa in two separated parts will be analyzed. First, based on the practice of the international court of justice, and then based on the guiding principles of the international law commission related to the principles applicable to the unilateral declarations of States capable of creating legal obligations.

This study tries to investigate and evaluate the fatwa from the standpoint of the international law. Therefore, our approach in writing this book has been in a way that is not beyond the terminology of the international law. Thus, at the beginning of the research we have used the principle of "description" in order to determine the status of the nuclear fatwa. On this basis, when we encounter an unknown legal institution in the international law, by resorting to the principle of description, first describe its nature and characteristics and then put it in one of the categories. The meaning of the category here is one of the valid legal frameworks under international law.

Accordingly the nuclear fatwa, based on what will be mentioned in detail, is in position of a unilateral legal act which has international authenticity under the international law. In this regard, the international law commission has codified specific provisions in the recognition and authentication of unilateral acts including the unilateral declarations. Circumstances of the terms governing on the nuclear fatwa as a document will be comparatively studied with the provisions of ILC principle guiding one by one. From the other aspect, one way to prove the authenticity of a document- under the international law- is to investigate the validity of the similar cases in practice of international judiciary.

Therefore, at the beginning of this section, with a brief introduction of some concerned topics of the law of evidence in international law, we will analyze the validity of unilateral acts from the standpoint of the international court of justice judgements and other international tribunals.

2.1. The Role of the Court in the Development of International law

International Court of Justice as the principal judicial organ of the United Nations and protector of the integrity of international law always tries to resolve disputes in accordance with applicable rights set forth in Article 38 of its statutes. This has not prevented the development of international law during the investigation of legal issues and disputes in terms of contentious and consultative jurisdiction. There should be a distinction between two concepts of legislation and the development of international law.

Article 24 of the Statute of the International Law Commission refers to the role of government policy in the development of international law as well as other factors and variables such as international courts decisions, especially the International Court of Justice opinion, as positive reasons or evidences of the existence of a rule of customary international law.

In other words, International Court attempts to extract and identify international law through its decisions. Controversies exist among the international legal experts in this regard. Broadly speaking, there have been two approaches in relation to this issue.

2.1.1. Traditional Approach

According to this approach, Article 38 of the Statute of the International Court of Justice includes the most recognized sources of international law. It refers to acts and not the creation of law. Article 38 of the Statute is faced some restrictions regarding the judicial decisions as a subsidiary source of international law. First, judicial decisions along with the "teachings of prominent writers of different nations" enjoy the subdominant feature. Accordingly, judicial decisions' duty is a tool which enables International Court to identify and apply the rules of customary international law. Secondly, it seems that this article allusion to Article 59 of the Statute, which is at the end of the 1 (d) of Article 38, eliminated the possibility of resorting to the doctrine of jurisprudence in international law. Therefore, judicial decisions have no value genuinely. However, as will be shown, there is no such restriction in practice.

2.1.2. Realistic Approach

According to this approach, one cannot deny that jurisprudence of the International Court of Justice is recognized as one of the sources of international law in practice. Side views of the Court on the interpretation of the rules are accepted as the best available understanding base of international law. They are also used as certain reasons.

This issue has been accepted not only by writers, but also

by governments and international courts. One of the trends in international investigations is that governments refer to previous judgments of the Court in order to prove their claims. In fact, they do not have any doubt about the validity. Governments may object to the issue in terms of lack of applicability of past decisions and not the lack of credibility. Articles 38 and 59 have never been cited. The other side claim has not been rejected. Fitzmaurice (judge) states that, over time, court decisions gain value and credit which separate opinions of dissenting judges do not have it (Morris, 1986, p. 345). Lauterpacht also cites several reasons for the court referring to his previous decisions (Lauterpacht, 1982, p. 14). He states that previous decisions of the Court are the factor of stability which affects future decisions in terms of legal and practical experience.

These decisions are regarded to be the reason for what the court considers as law. It will be a reliable statistics for the future position of the Court. Therefore, for practical reasons, these decisions show what international law is. In fact, they are largely similar to legal resources which have been mentioned in the first three paragraph of Article 38. In terms of form, they may only be considered as a subordinated instrument to determine the sources of law. However, the effect is the same (Ibid). The Court is also aware of the effects of its decisions beyond the parties. In the case of the Aegean Sea continental shelf, the Court stated that, however, under Article 59 of the Statute, court decisions have no binding effect beyond the parties and they are considered only in that specific case. Obviously, any comment of the Court in the case of 1928 law will also have consequences with respect to relations with other governments, with the exception of Greece and Turkey[1].

In the case of "Anglo-Iranian Oil Company", Alvarez also

---

1. Aegezn Sea Continental Shelf, I.C.J. Reports 1978, pp.16-17.

pointed to the Court's role in the development of international law. According to him, if the statute of the Court wants to limit his authority to the resolution of conflicts, the states will state it clearly. In that case, Court was considered merely the Court of International Arbitration, but the current Court is a Court of Justice. Given the dynamicity of international life, it has a dual role of rule declaration and development of rights. The first task is to settle disputes between states, as well as protecting the rights of the states in accordance with the Law of Nations. With regard to the second task of rights development, these tasks include deciding on existing rights, adjusting them, creating new concepts if needed. The second special task is justified by the dynamic character of international life[1].

Moreover, one cannot deny that the main sources of international law and judicial decisions branches are completely separated. They are very complex and affect each other. In many cases, judicial decisions establish the compilation basis of treaties. For example, Court decision of 1951 in the case of fishing (explaining the fact that drawing straight lines is the criteria to determine the width of the territorial sea) and the North Sea Continental Shelf decision of 1969 affected the formulation of Law of the Sea. Basic concepts such as armed attack and legitimate defense have crystallized in court procedures (for example, the case of Nicaragua)[2].

Therefore, it can be stated that court decisions have a very important role in the development of international rights. In some cases, they determine and interpret other sources of international

---

1. Anglo- Iranian Oil Co., I.C.J. Reports 1952, p.43, at 132,
2. About the ICJ role in development of international law see:
Jose Maria Ruda, Some of the Contribution of the International Court of Justice to the Development of International Law, Journal of International Law and Politics, Vol. 24, No. 1, pp. 35-68.

law as well. This is done in two ways. First, one of the tasks of the International Court of Justice is the identification of rules of customary international and their application toward the mentioned specific case. This task makes the court to identify a customary rule in the first step and introduce it. With this action, it can take part in the development of general international law. Secondly, in addition to international treaties and conventions, court may decide on the basis of general principles of international law.

In this case, to impose a general principle of law in a particular case, the Court will have to describe different aspects of the general legal principle. As a result, the scope of legal interpretation of that principle will be developed. This issue is more important especially when the Court is faced with the silence of the international treaties and customs. A glance at the mentioned function of ICJ indicates that the issuance of the nuclear fatwa and realization of a new procedure in States approach and utilization of sanctions policies in connection with weapons of mass destruction as well can underlie the development of international law. -

2.2. Sources of Law of evidence Proving Claim in International Court of Justice

In this article, those sources of international law which are used by International Court of Justice in the course of judicial duties in connection with fact-finding and proving the claims will be investigated. In the domestic legal system, there are usually compiled codes which are employed by judicial institutions to play their roles. For example, Articles 194 to 294 of the Civil Procedure Code of the Islamic Republic of Iran specify the rules governing the proof of claim. In international law, there are no compiled codes which can be used by the International Court. Moreover, international investigations are not equal in terms of procedure code. This means that each investigation is subject to its own conditions and requirements. For example, international arbitrations are different from international judicial investigations. Each international investigation depends largely on litigants. Dispute parties also affect investigation issues. However, over time, it was seen that rules and regulations have been gradually formed in jurisprudence and international arbitration in connection with matters of procedure generally and in connection with fact-finding and proving the case specifically.

Procedures of the Permanent Court and the International Court are parts of these procedures. Generally, sources of evidence proving claims in the international investigation can be divided into two main groups of written sources and unwritten sources. The main written source is founding documents and, in other words, the Statute of the International Courts and their investigation rules. The provisions contained in this resource usually express the general principles. They assign the details determination to the International Court. In addition to these resources, International Court must consider other unwritten sources. The most important unwritten sources are general principles of law and international jurisprudence.

On this basis, first I describe both categories of law of evidence in International Court of Justice to have a more meticulous evaluation from the act of nuclear fatwa.

2.2.1. Written Sources:

The main written regulations related to rules of evidence proving the claim can be found in Statutes and investigation rules of the International Court of Justice[1]. However, the court has

---

1. In the case of «military and paramilitary activities in and against Nicaragua», Court stated that «the regulations of the statutes and investigation rules in connection with offering the reason are designed

created written sources in other forms. Civil judicial procedures and administrative guidelines of the Court are among them. All these sources will be introduced in the following.

2.2.1.1. Principle Sources:

A. Statute of the International Court of Justice

The Statute of the International Court of Justice is the most important and most original document for duties of the Court. This Statute determines organizational issues, procedure and court powers. Broadly speaking, in the Statute, there are not many regulations related to the rules of evidence proving the claim. It contains Court general issues and power.

However, the Statute is the most important resource for decision-making on matters. It is a mother document. Therefore, other resources should be interpreted with respect to the provisions of the Statute. The provisions of the Statute are broad and flexible (Hygt, 1987, p. 356). With the division of the investigation procedure into two written and oral stages, the Statute regards the issues related to the Procedure Code such as rules of evidence proving the claim in two ways. Paragraph 5 of Article 43 has predicted the witnesses and experts hearings. In Article 44, the Court is allowed to visit the place to gain the reason. In a general prescription, Article 48 of the Statute has allowed the Court to issue some arrangements in order to handle the case. The court can decide on form and time of presentation of the arguments of each party. Moreover, this article authorizes the Court to make all the necessary arrangements related to finding the reason. Article 49 allows the Court to ask any document and explanation before

---

in order to ensure the proper execution of justice and fair and equal opportunity for both sides to comment on the claims of the other side.
Military and Paramilitary Activities in and against Nicaragua, I.C.J. Reports 1986,P. 16, at 26,para. 31.

court hearing of representatives. This Article specifies that, in case of failure, Court can formally consider the issue. Article 50 has made it possible to appoint an expert or expert group by the Court. Article 53 also specifies the conditions of the investigation in which one of the parties is absent. As it can be seen, Statute of the Court did not express significant provisions about rules of evidence proving the claim. This legislative gap regarding the proving issues such as standard proof of the claim and general issues can be seen more in the court.

2.2.1.2. Secondary Sources:

A. International Judicial Practice:

Article 19 of the Rules of proceedings allows the Court to determine its "internal judicial practice" by notices. Under this Article, the court civil judicial procedures should be determined according to the Statute through declaration that will be adopted by the Court. Accordingly, the court has approved its civil judicial procedures on 5th of July 1968. On April 12, 1976, in another statement, it has modified its civil judicial procedures. The declaration has 10 articles[1]. Prior to these two announcements, the court has regulated its civil judicial procedures in accordance to resolution of 20 February 1931 and amendment of 17 March 1936 of the Permanent Court. In the introduction of the Declaration of 1976, the Court states that if the Court finds the circumstances so required, it is free under certain conditions to deviate the resolution.

In the rules approved, the way of handling the issue is not mentioned. There are just the regulations addressing the issues raised by a case. According to Article 1 of this Declaration, Court

---

1. Resolution Concerning the Internal Judicial Practice of the Court, Adopted on 12 April 1976, Acts and Documents Concerning the Organization of the Court, No. 5, 1989, pp. 164-173.

judges can hold meeting on the sidelines of hearings. They can exchange their information and inform each other about their possible questions in order to apply paragraph 3 of Article 61 of the Rules of Court proceedings[1].

B. Practice Directions:

With regard to the increase of cases in the agenda of the International Criminal Court, the court has attempted to approve a set of rules known as "Practice Direction" in 2001 to solve practical problems in the course of investigations.[2] Gradually, the Court has attempted to complete this set. Court added other rules to this set for the last time on December 13, 2006. These rules have been developed with the aim to accelerate and facilitate the investigations of the Court. In connection with the legal basis for issuing these instructions, there is no clear conclusion. These rules can be justified according to the Court authority in Article 30 of the Statute. They can be considered as part of the Court's inherent powers. Accordingly, it can be noted that the governments of both sides are required to follow these rules. Among 12 practice directions issued by the Court, in some cases, there are some of the issues related to evidence and proof of the claim. In practice direction 1, it was stated that special agreement has no effect on the proof of claim. The practice direction number 2 asks the litigants to bring a summary of their arguments. The practice

---

1. For further information on the internal judicial practice of the Court See: Jennings, Sir Robert Y, The Internal Judicial Practice of the International Court of Justice, BYIL, Vol 59, 1988,31-47.

2. See: Arthur Watts, New Practice Directions of the International Court of Justice, The Law and Practice of International Courts and Tribunals; 2002, Vol. I, No. 2, pp. 247-256, Shabtai Rosenne, International Court of Justice: Practice Directions on Judges Ad Hoc; Agents, Counsel and advocates; And Submission of New Documents, LP1CT, Vol. 1, No. 2, pp. 223-245 and Arthur Watts, The I.C.J.›s Practice Directions of 30 July 2004, LPICT, 2004, Vol. 3, No. 2, pp. 385-394.

direction number 3 asks the litigants to bring a limited number of documents.

In practice direction 6, recalling the paragraph 1 of Article 60 of the rules of proceedings, it was stated that the oral hearing will be limited only to complain. The reason for this is that the competence and capability of lawsuit is the issue which should be investigated by the court itself. There is no need to hear the arguments of both sides. Practice direction number 9 implies the issue related to the documents registration with delay. This issue exists in paragraphs 1 and 2 of Article 56 of the Court proceeding rules as well. In connection with the registration of these documents, the Court has stated some restrictions. Practice direction No. 9 has determined the method of Implementation of paragraph 4 of Article 56 of the proceeding rules on the basis of oral hearings and documents which were not provided according to Article 43 of the Statute. Practice direction number 11 implies the limitations of telling the issue related to the issuance of temporary safeguarding in hearings. It can be stated that the Court has sought further restrictions to provide evidence and documents by governments.

As it can be seen, in International Court written sources, there are not many minor issues related to rules of evidence proving the claim. Only the general issues were highlighted. The main topics covered by these written sources are the evidence issues and the method to provide it. Basically, a lot of issues were not considered. For example, in these regulations, there is no article about proving, standard of proving or judicial value of any of the evidence. As will be shown in other parts of the research, the court has investigated such issues relying on other unwritten sources.

2.2.2. Unwritten Sources:

In addition to written sources, International Court of Justice uses other sources in investigation of issues related to rules of evidence proving the crime. The general principles of international law and international judicial procedure are among these sources.

2.2.2.1. General Principles of International law:

Paragraph (c) of Article 38 of the Statute of the Court implies "the general principles of law recognized by civilized nations". During the investigation of claims, the Court uses this resource. However, topics have been proposed concerning the scope and meaning (Bin Cheng, 1953, p. 536). Placing the general principles of law as a source of international law in Article 38 of the Statute of the Court has been done to "complete the international legal system". International law is more uncertain compared to domestic law. Most international lawyers agree that the purpose of insertion of the general principles of law is to prevent the legal gap. In practice, Court pays no attention to the "civilized nations". It can be stated that, in the view of the Court, all countries are civilized nations. These principles do not belong to any specific legal system. They are common in all systems.

Bin Chang, in one of the most famous written works related to the general principles of law, considers three special tasks for this legal source. First, the general principles of law are the source of many legal rules which express these principles. Second, the general principles of law are considered to be the guidance of legal orders which inspire the interpretation and implementation of legal rules. Third, in the absence of law, the facts of the case are applied. In legal systems, such as international law in which the written rules are limited, the third special task of the general legal principles is very important. It plays an important part in defining the legal relations among States (Ibid., P. 390).

Permanent Court and International court of Justice pay

attention to the general legal principles contained in Article 38 of the Statute of the Court. Permanent Court never mentioned this Article. It always spoke about it in a vague and ambiguous form. In some cases, Permanent Court Citations can be classified in the principles of customary international law and the general principles of law of the paragraph (c) of Article 38 of the Statute[1]. International Court pays attention to this resource in several cases explicitly[2], but it pays attention to this resource in a lot of cases without any citations[3].

Although there was no hierarchy between sources of international law and the issues of contractual rights and customary law are paid much attention, international rights (international treaties and conventions) have a secondary character. However, in connection with the rules of evidence proving the claim, the general principles of law must be considered one of the main sources. In the case of "some German interests in Upper Church"

---

1. See: Mavrommatis Jerusalem Concessions, P.C.I.J., Series A, No. 5, p. 30; Certain German Interests in Polish Upper Silesia, P.C.I.J., Series A, No. 6, p. 19; Article 3,Paragraph 2, of the Treaty of Lausanne, P.C.I.J., Series B, No. 12, p. 132; Certain German Interests in Polish Upper Silesia (Merits), P.C.I.J., Series A, No. 7, p. 22; Factory at Chorzow (Jurisdiction), P.C.I.J., Series A, No. 9, p. 311; Interpretation of the Greco-Turkish Agreement of December 1st, 1926, P.C.I.J., Series B, No. 16, pp. 20 and 25, Factory at Chorzow (Merits), P.C.I.J., Series A, No. 17, p. 29.

2. See: Right of Passage over Indian Territory, I.C.J.. Reports 1960, pp. 6,43; South West Africa, I.C.J. Reports 1966, pp. 6, 47, para. 91; North Sea Continental Shelf I.C.J.. Reports 1969, pp. 3, 21, para. 17; Avena and other Mexican Nationals, I.C.J. Reports 2004, pp. 12, 61, Para. 127.

3. Corfu Channel, I.C.J. Reports 1949, pp. 4, 18; Barcelona Traction, Light and Power Company, Ltd., I.C.J. Reports 1970, pp. 3, 37, para 50; Application offor Review of Judgment No. 158 of the United Nations Administrative Tribunal, I.C.J. Reports 1973, pp. 166, 177, paras. 29 and 30; Difference Relating to Immunity from Legal Process of a Special Rapporteur of the Commission on Human Rights, I.C.J. Reports 1999, pp. 62,88, para. 63.

when dealing with a matter of procedure, the Permanent Court put the general principles of law near the provisions of the Statute and Rules of Court proceedings[1].

2.2.2.2. International Jurisprudence:

Observing Article 59, paragraph 1 (d) of Article 38 of the Statute, has introduced judicial decisions as incidental tools for setting the rules. In the past, justifying the use of previous judicial decisions (including the decisions of the Court) was very difficult. Today, their important position has been identified by the Court and writers. This regulation does not show the Court commitment to the doctrine of judicial procedures as it is in the common-law legal system. In the Statute of the Permanent Court, there is exactly the same regulation. However, this regulation does not prevent the court to use its previous findings in reaching its decisions. In any case, the existence of convincing reason of the Permanent Court can deviate from its previous practice. Accordingly, in many cases, the Permanent Court cited the principles of jurisdiction, procedure and substantive in its previous opinions. Hereby, the Permanent Court created the organized approaches in connection with many legal fields.

In this regard, judicial decisions considered by the Court can be divided into three categories; the Permanent Court judicial procedure, Court procedure and procedures of other international courts. Among these cases, Court usually pays much attention to its judicial decisions and Permanent Court judicial procedure. It rarely refers to the decisions of other international courts.

A. Jurisprudence of Other International Tribunals:

In practice, the Court has no tendency to rely on judicial procedure of other international courts. A former employee

---

1. Certain German Interests in Polish Upper Silesia, P.C.I.J., Series A, No. 6, p. 19.

of the Court claims that, in the Court, there are unwritten rules according to which Court should only refer to its judicial procedure. However, in some cases, the Court also refers to procedures of other courts.

In addition to cases in which another court decision forms the topic[1], Court on various occasions has referred to other international opinions. In some cases, in general, Court refers to them using some terms such as "procedures,"[2] "arbitration court decisions"[3], "international decisions"[4] or "international judicial procedures"[5]. In some cases, Court specifically referred to these ideas. In the case of "land, sea and border's dispute", the Court Branch considered decision of 1917 of the Central American Court of Justice as a supplementary tool[6]. On several occasions, the Court cited ALamaba's arbitration vote[7] of 1872 and Britain and France arbitration[8] of 1977. Moreover, recently, in the case

---

1. *See e. g.* Arbitral Award Made by the King of Spain on 23 December 1960, *I.C.J. Report 1960, p. 192;* Arbitral Award of 31 July 1989, *I.C.J. Report 1991, p. 53.*
2. *Lotus*, P.C.I.J. Series A, No. 10, p. 26.
3. *Factory at Chorzow (Merits),* P.C.I.J., Series A, No. 17, p. 47; Gulf of Maine, I.C.J. Reports 1984, pp. 246, 290, para. 83 and Arrest Wan-ant of 11 April 2000, I.C.J. Reports 2002, pp. 3, 31-32, para. 76.
4. *Corfu Channel,* I.C.J. Reports 1949, pp. 4, 8 and Nottebohm, I.C.J. Reports 1955,pp. 4, 21-22
5. Constitution of the Maritime Safety Committee of the IMCO, *I.C.J. Reports 1960, pp. 150, 169*
6. I.C.J. Report 1992, p. 601, para. 403.
7. Nottebohm (Preliminary Objection), *I.C.J. Reports 1953, pp. III, 119 and* Applicability of the Obligation to Arbitrate under Section 21 of the United Nations Headquarters Agreement of 26 June 1947, *I.C.J. Reports 1947,*
I.C.J. Reports 1988. pp.12, 34, para. 57.
8. See: Continental Shelf (Tunisia/Libyan Arab Jamahiriya), I.C.J. Reports 1982, pp.18, 57, para. 66 and 79, para. 109; Delimitation of the Maritime Boundaiy in the Gulf of Maine, I.C.J. Reports 1984, pp.

of the Convention on Genocide, the Court finds no shame in reference to the International Criminal Court of Yugoslavia. In the case, reference to Yugoslavia court decisions was conducted as the reason, not as a substantive judicial procedure. In one case, Yugoslavia court procedure was criticized.

B. Jurisprudence of Permanent Court of International Justice:

In connection with court reference to past decisions of the Permanent Court, there is no obstacle. The Court has repeatedly endorsed the Permanent Court judicial procedure. The court position is different from the Permanent Court's from an organizational perspective, but their judicial procedures are considered to be the same. The Court had considered the past decisions of the Permanent Court. In order to prevent confusion in appealing to the Permanent Court judicial procedure in San Francisco Conference, it was tried to reinstate the numbering of the Statute of the Permanent Court. In this regard, in 1984, in the case of Nicaragua, the Court stated that "the primary concern of the Statute draft producers to maintain the integrity between the Court and the former Court as much as possible"[1]. Therefore, the Court made no distinction between its decisions and the Permanent Court's. In this regard, Winiarski (judge) has stated that "since starting to work, the Court had considered the continuity of tradition, judicial procedure and practices".

Guerrero, the last chairman of the former Court, was the first chairman of the Court. With limited and insignificant reforms,

---

246, 203, para. 92, 302-303, para. 123 and 324, para. 187; Maritime Delimitation in the Area between Greenland and Jan Mayen, I.C.J. Reports 1993, pp. 38, 58, para 46, 51-52, para. 51, 62, para. 55 and 67, para. 66; Maritime Delimitation and Territorial Questions between Qatar and Bahrain, I.C.J. Reports 2001, pp. 40, 114-*115, para. 247;* Land and Maritime Boundary betweenCameroon and Nigeria, *I.C.J. Reports 2002, pp. 303, 432, para. 270.*

1. I.C.J. Reports 1984, p. 407, para. 32.

the court has adopted the investigation rules of the former Court. Most importantly, without commitment to the Stare Decisis as a principle or rule, the court usually uses the former Court decisions. The result has been the remarkable unity of procedure which is an important factor in the development of international law[1]. Accordingly, the Court repeatedly referred to the Permanent Court judicial procedure in its decisions. The main reason for this is the official successor of the Permanent Court[2].

C. Jurisprudence of International Court of Justice:

In reference to its previous decisions, the Court does not hesitate. These decisions have gradually become one of the main documents of the Court. In other words, in addition to various factors, the court paid attention[3] to "Case-Law of the Court ". It has repeatedly cited this procedure. These decisions include pleading votes and advices. The results of an investigation show that the International Court of Justice referred to its previous decisions in 26 percent of cases between 1948 and 2002. For example, the court referred to its previous decisions more than 28

---

1. Interpretation of Peace Treaties with Bulgaria, Hungary and Romania, Second Phase, I.C.J. Reports 1950, pp. 232-233.
2. Condition of Admission of a State to Membership of a State to Membership in the United Nations (Article 4 of Charter), I.C.J. Reports 1948, p. 63, Corfu Channel, I.C.J. Reports 1949, pp. 4 and 24; Reparation for Injuries Suffered in the Services of the United Nations, I.C.J. Reports 1949, p. 182; Effects of Awards of Compensation Made by the United Nations Administrative Tribunal, I.C.J. Reports1954,p.56;Competence of the General Assembly for the Admission of a State to the United Nations, I.C.J. Reports 1950, p. 8; Rights of Nationals of the United Nations of America in Morocco ,I.C.J. Report 1952, p. 206; Certain Norwegian Loans, I.C.J. Reports 1957, pp. 23-24; Barcelona Traction, Light and Power Company, Limited, Preliminary Objections, I.C.J. Reports 1964, p. 46; Nuclear Tests, I.C.J. Reports 1974, p. 270, para. 54.
3. Application for Review of Judgment No. 273 of the United Nations Administrative Tribunal, I.C.J. Reports1982, p. 355, para. 57

times only in 3 pages of advisory theory of 2004.

As highlighted above, according to article 38 of ICJ Statute, nuclear fatwa can be considered as both written source -and based on international judicial practice and general principles-, unwritten source as well for law of evidence proving claim in international tribunals.

2.3. Principles Governing the Production, Admissibility and Evaluation of the Evidence in the International Court of Justice:

In the knowledge of law, speaking about the reason is possible when an event leads the mind to reality. In other words, when the mind becomes able to reach the unknown through its findings, that sign is called reason whether an external event or a provision of law. Therefore, reason is sometimes used synonymously with cause and analogy. It was said that whatever persuade the spirit for the existence of truth is reason. In this way, the legal and judicial mean of proof is not taken away. Reason is the signs of the existence of truth which is disputed (Katouzian, 1384, p. 20). In international investigations, dealing with reason is slightly different from internal law. In internal systems, there are certain rules and regulations in connection with reason according to which the accepted formats of a document are defined as reason[1]. In international investigations, there is no specific and precise definition for reason. "The flexibility of international investigations, the tendency for resistance against the special rules of applicable evidence in domestic legal systems makes

---

1. To define the concept of reason, legal systems of countries have taken different approaches. Some systems have clearly declared the acceptable formats for reason. Others are more flexible. In Article 1258, Iranian Civil Code has announced a variety of reasons (Confession, written documents, testimonies and oath).

the concept of reason much wider in international investigation (Kazzazi, 1996, p. 180).

The International Court, generally, reason is "the documents which are presented by one of the parties in accordance with his initiative or the Court request to prove a claimed fact or a claimed legal right"[1]. Another point is that the detailed categories in the domestic legal systems have no important role in International proceedings especially in claims of International Court of Justice. The term reason is referred to as all the tools and templates to prove a fact.

2.3.1. Principles Governing the Process of Fact-finding in International Court of Justice:

Generally, two basic principles can be introduced in relation with offering, accepting and evaluating the evidence in International Court of Justice. They are also applicable in other international courts. First, unlike national courts, the government can provide any evidence or reason. In other words, there is no acceptable evidence and unacceptable evidence in particular sense (Principle of freedom of the parties in presenting the reason). Secondly, in acceptance and evaluation of the evidence presented, the Court enjoys an extensive freedom (Principle of Court freedom in reception and assessment of the reason)[2]. Gradually, in practice, it can be seen that all these principles have accepted restrictions as follows.

---

1. A Dialogue at the Court, Proceedings of the I.C.J./UNITAR Colloquium held on the Occasion of the Sixtieth Anniversary of the International Court of Justice, at the Peace Palace on 10 and 11 April 2006, Edited and Published by the Registry of the Court, p. 25.
2. For more information see: Rudiger Wolfrum, Talking and Assesing Evidence in International Adjudication, in: Malick Ndiaye, Rudiger Wolfrum, Law of the Sea, Environment and settlement of Disputes: Liber Amicrum Judge Thomas A. Mensah, 2007, pp. 341-356.

2.3.1.1. The Parties Freedom to Produce Evidence:

In all provisions of the Statute and rules of Court proceedings, the kind of evidence confirmed by the Court is not specified. The entire form of the evidence is assigned to the governments. Evidence may include the governments' official documents, national legislation, map, report of international organizations, the United Nations resolution, media and newspapers content and government officials and individuals' comments. International Court of Justice has interpreted the lake of the rules defined in the Statute in relation to the type and form of evidence in a way that a litigant can present any suitable reason within the time specified by the Court. In practice, the Court considers few restrictions for litigants, but, in some cases, it uses its power to reject the proposed reason (Duward V, 1999, p. 184).

2.3.1.2. Court Freedom to Accept and Evaluate Evidence:

The freedom of parties to provide evidence has the analogy of the freedom of court to accept and evaluate the evidence presented by parties[1]. Court is not limited to any specific evidence system. It is considered to be the final authority to accept and evaluate the evidence. It has an extensive power. This does not mean that the Court can act arbitrarily. The Court has developed a set of rules which needs to be developed based on the mentioned issues and problems of evidence in some cases[2]. When assessing the evidence, Court even acts freer compared to Admission stage. This is largely similar to the internal regulations of countries[3]. This

---

1. For more information see: Witenberg, La Theorie des Preuve devant Ies Juridictions Internationales, Recueil Des Cours, Tome 56, 1936, p. 65.
2. A Dialogue at the Court, Proceedings of the I.C.J./UNITAR Colloquium held on the Occasion of the Sixtieth Anniversary of the International Court of Justice, at the Peace Palace on 10 and 11 April 2006, Edited and Published by the Registry of the Court, p. 26.
3. See: Duward V. Sandifer, *op. cit.*, pp. 15-16

means that, to determine the burden of proof, it didn't determine any rule and criteria. It makes decision according to the conditions of each reason.

Nuclear fatwa as an international[1] official State act is presentable in international tribunals and in this respect Islamic Republic of Iran has freedom to produce evidence.

2.4. Statements by Officials or Governmental Institutions:

In the last decades, we have witnessed a revolution in the field of international trade tools. This has led to facilitate the access to high-ranking representatives of the government (Watts, 1994, p. 114). These groups of data such as press conference, joint statement, Radio and TV interviews and lecture at the national, regional and international institutions are used to confirm the interpretations and claims. .70 Referring to these statements is based on the fact that no one can benefit from his contradictory behavior toward others[2]. In other words, a litigant cannot deny the truth after confessing it (Estoppel Rule). Confession is a truth or a possible right. It is performed by an international document such as treaty, specific agreements and exchange of notes. It can be understood by representatives' behavior and speech.

However, the only time to consider an issue as a confession is, first, when it is expressed explicitly. Secondly, confession should be voluntarily and unconditionally. Finally, referring to the confession must be made in accordance with the principle of good faith. The statements which don't have all or some of these elements cannot be referred according to the Estoppel rule. There are no definitive binding. They can have a degree of proving value (Bowett, 1957, p.

---

1. Especially based on its registration in United Nations.
2. allegcins controria non audiendus est

202). Officials' statements are presented before the International Court of Justice in two ways[1]. Statements made by government officials were referred before the dispute. This statement is used as a supporting reason for a fact. For example, an official involved in the conclusion of an international treaty states his understanding of the regulation of the treaty. In fact, he explains the inherent obligations of his country according to that treaty. In the International Court of Justice, appealing to government officials' statements is done with two goals. With referring to officials of other governments, governments are seeking to prove the facts which have been disputed. In some cases, officials' statements are referred to as the reason of a commitment or an International right in terms of the sea area or territory. In this section, the Court Procedure will be investigated in relation to both groups.

2.4.1. Political Officials' Statements as Proving Evidence of Fact or International Responsibility of States:

As stated, in some cases, the litigants refer to other side government. There are always these documents in Court. In fact, one of the common ways in Court is referring to such statements. However, the method of dealing with these evidences is not always the same. It depends on the conditions and circumstances of each case. The existence of such statements does not indicate a fact. It can be stated that there is a kind of direct relationship between the level of official and the degree of transparency of statements. In other words, the higher level of official causes clearer expression. The relationship between the expressed issue and administrative

---

1. In this section, the importance of political officials› statements is presented. The next section belongs to the role of these materials in the formation of international rules, especially the rules of customary. Cases in which the political officials› statements are referred to as the commitment reason are paid attention.

tasks of official is important. In the case of Minco, in order to prove its sovereignty over Minco, England referred to the French ambassador's note of June 12, 1820. At one of the tables, the letter of Maritime Minister is presented as English. France claimed that Britain cannot rely on this letter. First, it was presented during the negotiations between the parties. Secondly, negotiations did not lead to any agreement. However, the Court rejected the France argument. According to Court, this document is not an offer or a compromise during negotiations. This is the facts presented by the ambassador of France. Therefore, this statement should be considered as reason of official views[1].

In the case of "military and paramilitary activities in and against Nicaragua", the value of officials' statements was presented. The Court stated that the contents of the Court include the statements of governments' representatives and high ranking officials. Some of the statements are presented at the formal institutions of government or a regional or international organization. Other comments were presented during press conferences or interviews which are reported by local and international press. The Court opinion is that such statements by senior political figures have special value if they are confirmed by the highest authority. However, it is natural that such statements shall be treated with caution. Article 53 and other basis cannot justify the selective approach which ruins the conformance of court procedure and primary task of equality between the parties. The court should consider the situation according to which the statements have been express publicly. The Court cannot value them equally without considering the way of their presentation. The statements in a national or international official publication are not the same.

It should be considered that whether the text of the official

---

1. The Minquiers and Ecrehos, (France/United Kingdom), *I.C.J. Reports 1953, p. at 71.*

statements is in the native language of the speaker or it is based on the presented translation. It should be considered that whether these statements are presented through recorded official correspondence or not. In some cases, the court should interpret these statements to ensure the confirmation of a fact[1]. The Court also stated that "the court considers the statements to be very important". The Court should scrutinize the declaration. In this case, two witnesses were Nicaraguan officials.

The United States registered the testimony of the foreign minister. Court classified these evidences in "special groups" (ibid). In connection with the legal effects of such declarations, the Court stated some points. First, according to Court, such statements can be considered as the reason of the accuracy of the facts. Secondly, such statements indicate that these reasons are related to the government which its officials stated them. Thirdly, they can be considered as the reason for description of the facts. The Court considers the statements which are contrary to the views of the government very important (ibid).

The important point stated by the court in this case is that the Court is not limited to contents that mentioned by litigants. In its path, in search of truth, the Court may consider the statements by representatives of the claim in international organizations and resolutions adopted or discussed in these organizations in the case of thematic relationship (ibid). It is not clear that this conclusion of the Court has the general feature. In fact, In order to perform its task, the court acted upon the Article 53 of the Statute to ensure the reasonableness of the subject. With this argument, while expressing the availability of a published document titled "Revolution Beyond our Border", the court has stated that, with regard to the specific circumstances of the case, the information

---

1. *Military and Paramilitary Activities in and against Nicaragua*, I.C.J. Reports 1986, p. at. 41, paras. 64-65.

of this document will be used (ibid).

In a few cases, according to the statements of United States officials, the court has accepted some facts of the case. For example, referring to the television interview of President Reagan on May 28, 1984, the court attributed the mining of Nicaragua's harbors to the country (ibid., P. 47). Reagan press conference on October 19 of 1983 was considered to be the reason for accepting the role of United States in attacks against Corinto by the court. In this case, the Court emphasized that this does not mean the direct participation of US troops in the attacks (ibid., P. 49). In the case of "oil platform», to assign the attack on an American ship named "Sea Isle City" to the troops of Islamic Republic of Iran, United States referred to the statement by President of Iran(Ayatollah Khamenei) which was made three months before the attack. The speech expressed that the United States will be attacked if it doesn't leave the region. In this regard, without careful evaluation of expressions, the Court stated that this reason is not enough[1]. There was not any causal relationship between the threats and criminal action. The court opinion was criticized by American judge[2].

Moreover, recently, in the case of "territorial and maritime dispute between Nicaragua and Honduras in the Caribbean Sea", Nicaragua referred to the note of Minister of Foreign Affairs of Honduras of May 3, 1982 to prove the absence of an agreed boundary between the two countries. After reviewing the notes, the Court stated that it was considered the Honduras official point of view about the maritime border between the two countries. Accordingly, Honduras accepted that, at that time, there was no

---

1. Oil Platforms (Islamic Republic of Iran v. United States of America), *I.C.J. Reports, 2003, p. at 190, para. 60.*
2. Separate Opinion of Judge Buergenthal, *Ibid,* p. at 287, para. 42.

maritime delimitation[1].

2.4.2. Political Officials' Statements as the Basis for the Acceptance of International Obligations or Recognition of International Rights of Other States:

As was expressed, political officials' statements can prove a fact and create a commitment for a government. In this regard, there are some examples. In Permanent Court, the credibility of a country's political officials' statements was presented. In the case of "the legal status of Eastern Greenland", Denmark referred to Norwegian Foreign Minister's statements to prove its sovereignty over all sections of East Greenland.

In that case, in response to the question of Chief Minister of Denmark about his assessment of the outlook for the Norwegian government position, Norwegian Foreign Minister has stated that the Norwegian government will not present any problems in this regard. This article was included in the minutes of Ministry of Norway. After considering the issue, Court stated that Norway government is committed to avoid from challenging Denmark sovereignty regarding all of Eastern Greenland territory[2]. In Court's view (a response with such quality by foreign minister on behalf of his government in response to a foreign government diplomatic ambassador's request, related to the issue which lies in his area, is necessary for the minister followed government)[3]. In the case of (Eastern Greenland Legal Status), Permanent Court had access to the proceedings of Norway foreign minister's statements through that country Foreign Office archive. Considering the offered rule by Permanent Court in the mentioned case, this

---

1. Territorial and Maritime Dispute between Nicaragua and Honduras in the Caribbean Sea (Nicaragua v. Honduras), *I.C.J. Reports 2006, para. 257*
2. See: Garner, The International Binding Force of Oral Declarations, AJIL, Vol.27, pp. 493-497.
3. *Legal Status of Eastern Greenland*, P.C.I.J. Ser. A/B, No. 53, p. at 70.

question is posed that if there is no access to the proceedings of a political authority's statements, how it could be documented?

Related to this issue, One of the authors has pointed out practical problem of resort to Courts authority and international courts based on the request from the parties to represent concerned proves, and form their vantage point, when the government having the proceedings avoids, courts can view the fault of this county as a kind of judicial deduction. Also, in the case of (refuge), each of the parties adduced to formal declarations and reports ascribed to the governmental constitutions of opposite side to proof existence of common rule related to return.Cambodia indicated formal declarations of Peru foreign office on October 13 and 26, 1948, and also Peru mentioned consultative committee report of Colombia foreign office issued on September 2, 1937. Nevertheless, Court in that case preferred to ignore these statements. Form Court's view (these evidences express views that conflict with present ideas of litigant governments. Court that its task in the present case is to exert international law cannot attach Decisive Importance to these evidences)[1].

The issue of importance of governmental formal statements in causing international commitment was also posed in the cases of (nuclear experiments). After the case of New Zealand and Australia from France regarding nuclear experiments, French authorities as defender stated some statements. Considering this issue , it can be referred to the statements of the President on July 25, 1974; Defense minister on August 16, 1974; Foreign minister on September 25, 1974 at the United Nations General Assembly ; Defense minister of France on October 11,1974. Among these statements, Court viewed the President of France as the most fundamental[2]. 92. The President of France during a press

---

1. *Asylum, (Columbici/Peru)*, I.C.J. Reports 1950, p. at 278.
2. *Nuclear Tests Case, (New Zealand v. France)*, I.C.J. Reports 1974, p. at

conference noted: (Regarding the issue of nuclear experiments, you are aware that the prime minister publicly talked about this issue at National Assembly during introducing government programs. He specified that nuclear experiments of France will be continued. I also clarified that this epoch will be the last one and thus the members of cabinet completely has got aware of our goals…) (ibid)

Court regarding the impacts of these statements declared(without any doubt, concerning his tasks as the head of government, his public correspondence and statements, whether oral or written, will be considered as a part of international doings of France). Court also pointed out the general consistency quality of the stated statements by French authorities including Defense minister's statements of France and accordingly concluded that regardless of the statements format, with respect to their aim and condition of expressing, it can be indicated that (these statements will cause a commitment for the government) (ibid) Accordingly and regarding that France government (the end of atmosphere nuclear experiments in Pacific Ocean) with this commitment, in fact, asked for complainant of accepted case, Court avoided from dealing more with different aspects of the case (Ibid, p. 478). Court way in this case indicates that court has noticed to two factors of aim and condition leading to expressing of authorities' statements to achieve the conclusion that a government is committed to do something due to its authorities' formal statements (Ibid, p.472). Of course when interpreting these statements, strict interpretation approach must be taken (Ibid, p.473).

On the contrary, court in the case of (Border Dispute), by adducing to this issue that the expressing condition of Mali President's statements at a press interview has not been indicative of the intention of creating commitment, avoided from giving

---

474, para. 51.

obligatory aspect impact to his statements[1]. Also, joint declarations can be considered as tools to determine law and commitments of parties in Court. For example, Greece in the case of (Aegean continental shelf) adduced to a joint declaration issued after the prime ministers meeting of this country and Turkey.

Greece reasoned that this declaration aim is to refer the disagreement between these two countries to Court. Hereof, Court announced: (There has been no rule in international law that, based on it, a joint declaration cannot be considered as the basis of international agreement for referring disagreement to arbitration or judicial settlement institution). But it is important that Court considers exact statements of joint declaration and specific condition leading to issuing of the declaration[2]. Qatar government in the case of (determination of maritime and Territorial boundary between Qatar and Bahrain) adduced to 1990 the proceedings as the basis of competence. Oppositely, Bahrain argued that in the form of these proceedings no commitment has been obligated in legal conception. Concerning this court announced: (therefore, 1990 the proceedings are the Confirmation of commitments that already had got irrevocable. These proceedings gave King Fahd the task to try to find a solution for the disagreement in 6 months; and Finally that the condition which can be resorted to Court after May 1990 has mentioned in them.

In results, contrary to Bahrain argument, these proceedings have not viewed as a simple record of the session; they merely do not state discussions and is not summary of agreed and disagreed points. They display the commitments that the parties have expressed their satisfaction towards them. Thus, according to international law bring about law and commitments for the

---

1. Frontier Dispute, I.C.J. Reports 1986, pp. 265-266, para?
2. Aegean Sea Continental Shelf, I.C.J. Reports 1978, p. 40, at 39, Para. 96.

parties)¹. Bahrain in that case argued that the signers of this document did not intend to conclude such a mandatory agreement.

Bahrain adduced to the statements of Bahrain foreign minister on May 21, 1992 to confirm this own claim. According to this evidence, Bahrain foreign minister had declared that (I did never think that I with signing these proceedings commit Bahrain to a legally mandatory agreement. Also, he, hinting at Bahrain constitution process regarding joining to international agreements, stated that he basically has not have permission to sign such an international agreement and in fact he conceived that he signs just a document containing political mutual understanding. Court, rejecting these statements, stated:(Bahrain foreign minister after signing such a text cannot consequently announce that his intention has been to join to a (declaration containing political mutual understanding) and not an international agreement (Ibid, p. 122). This approach of Court has been greatly criticized by some authors. most of these criticism are related to that court has not tried much in its view regarding the translation of the mutual understanding record Arabic text to English and analyzed facts of the case well and court must have applied kind of (subject-matter skepticism) in this case (Mc Hugo, 1997, p.171).

Also, issue of capacity of creating international commitment by national authorities (other than foreign minister, head of reign and head of the government) was posed recently. Congo in that case adduced to genocide Convention IX Article to proof Court competency. Nevertheless, concerning Rwanda reservation at the time of passage, there was a question that whether the defendant has restored this reservation or not? Concerning this, Congo adduced to statements of Rwanda Ministry of justice at 61th session The United Nations Human rights Commission on March

---

1. Maritime Delimitation and Territorial Questions between Qatar and Bahrain (Qatar v. Bahrain), *I.C.J. Reports 1994, at p. 121, para. 25.*

17, 2005.

At that session, he indicated that a few number of human law agreements are not passed by this country that will be ratified soon. In addition, Rwanda will restore its own reservations towards human law agreements in the future. Kong government adducing to these statements argued that Rwanda has restores its own reservation towards 1948 Convention mentioned Article and accordingly court has competence to view. Oppositely, Rwanda argued that it has never done any measures related to this issue.

Concerning the statements of justice ministry of this country, it also adduced that first, he has never referred to any specific reservations and additionally that return time is also undetermined. Secondly, the statements of justice ministry like the sentences of a foreign minister and or the head of the reign does not cause international obligation for Rwanda government. Court regarding this , referring to own prior judicial approach[1], announced (one of basic rules of international law is that the head of government , the head of reign and foreign minister merely represent their own government trough accomplishing their tasks including doing of unilateral practices on behalf of that government that has impact of international commitments .

Court, in addition, reminds that this common rule, regarding agreement conclusion, has been inserted in article 7 paragraph 2 Vienna Convention on the Law of Treaties. However, in Court' vantage point, with increase of modern international exchanges,

---

1. Nuclear Tests (Australia *v.* France), *I.C.J. Reports 1974, pp. 269-270, paras. 49-51;* Application of the Convention on the Prevention and Punishment of the Crime of Genocide (Bosnia and Herzegovina *v.* Yugoslavia), Preliminary Objections, *I.C.J. Reports 1996 (II), p. 622, para. 44;* Arrest Warrant of 11 April 2000 (Democratic Republic of the Congo **v.** Belgium), I.C.J. Reports 2002, pp. 21-22, para. 53; see also *Legal Status of Eastern Greenland (Denmark v Norway),* 1933, P.C.I.J., Series A/B No. 53, p. 71.

other persons who act on behalf of their governments are also possible to be authorized in obligating their followed government in areas under their competencies.[1]) Thus, Court admitted that Rwanda justice minister can obligate his followed government under some conditions; particularly that human rights is one of the issues that lie in justice minister competency area (ibid).

Then, Court dealt with examining legal impacts of Rwanda justice minister's statements. Court to determine legal impacts of such declarations, according to the approach of Court, should assess real content and as well the condition leading to the presentation of them[2]. In addition, Court pointed out that these statements in order to cause commitment should be clear and well-defined[3]. Accordingly, Court after assessment of Rwanda justice minister's statement sentences reached to the conclusion that legal obligation cannot be elicited from these statements for his followed government[4].

Furthermore, Court in its verdict in the case of (sovereignty towards Pedra/ Branca Batu Puteh, mid rock and south bump) to determine sovereignty over conflicting island noted greatly to September 21, 1953 letter of the headman of Republic foreign ministry (Malaysia self- government). The headman of Republic foreign ministry in this letter had stated that Johor government does not have any ownership claim to Pesra Branca Island. Court believed that (this letter and its interpretations has key importance

---

1. Armed Activities on the Territory of the Congo, (New Application: 2002) (DRC v. Rwanda), I.C.J. Reports 2006, paras. 46-47.
2. Nuclear Tests (Australia v. France), I.C.J. Reports 1974, p. 269, para. 51; Frontier *Dispute (Burkina Faso/Republic of Mali),* I.C.J. Reports 1986, pp. 573-574, paras. 39-40.
3. Nuclear Tests (Australia v. France) (New Zealand v. France), I.C.J. Reports 1974, p. 267, para. 43; p. 269, para. 51; p. 472, para. 46; p. 474, para. 53.
4. Armed Activities on the Territory of the Congo, (New Application: 2002), (DRC v.Rwanda), I.C.J. Reports 2006, paras. 51-53.

in determining the parties perception about sovereignty over Pedra Branca/Pulau Batu Puteh.¹)

Court ,rejecting Malaysia argument related to the country (ibid)ministry headman incompetency, announced that the response of Republic government agent in 1953 indicates that this country's view from that time has been not to have any ownership claim to Pedra Branca/Pulau Batu Puteh island (ibid) and accordingly, put aside two centuries of effective sovereignty over this area. The Court, consequently, in this case, surveying the approach and function of the parties after 1953, announced that sovereignty over island belonged to Singapore. As it mentioned, based on ICJ judiciary practice, as evidence, official authorities' statements are representable before ICJ, accordingly, nuclear fatwa as a well-defined act, deals with stopple principle.

2.5. Guiding Principles Applicable to Unilateral Declarations of States Capable of Creating Legal Obligations and its Comparative Study with Nuclear Fatwa

Regarding the legal Status of Nuclear Fatwa, as an internationally unilateral legal act, first its position is briefly explained under international law and then the study of Fatwa and ILC related codification is examined comparatively. Generally, a unilateral act of state is a clear manifestation of the will which is created by a State with the purpose of generating legal results in connection with the subjects of the international law. States, based on the various needs, make many unilateral acts. Accordingly, the issuance of a unilateral act by a State does not need the specific formalities concerning the law of treaties, and a State can obtain its aim in a short time. The importance of unilateral acts of States can be

---

1. Sovereignty over Pedra Branca/Pulau Batu Puteh, Middle Rocks and South Ledge (Malaysia/Singapore), I.C.J. Reports 2008, para. 203.

observed in the International Court of Justice judgement in case of France Nuclear Test and also in 51/160, the resolution of GA whereby asked ILC to analyze more about the several legal aspects of unilateral acts of States.

Regardless of being unilateral or not, every legal act has its specific condition. A legal act means an action that has been manifested by the State will in order to create some legal results. These acts, can be appeared in various forms including: multilateral, bilateral and unilateral. If an action is done in a one-sided way, it is categorized in sort of unilateral acts and in case of two or more States participation is classified among the bi or multilateral acts of states. The unilateral legal act itself is divided into two concepts: general and specific; specific act relates to the act of States whereas the general act includes the act of organization (resolution). The unilateral acts of States can be issued in several form such as; recognition, promise and commitment, protest and silence, forfeiture (waiver), declaration or statement, collective act, notice or announcement.

The acceptance of a new member state by the other States is usually manifested by a unilateral act. The manifestation of an objection to a specific situation, case or a forming practice is usually operationalized by the issuance of a unilateral act which indicates the protest of a State to something. Based on the rule of "the silence gives consent" silence in case of making the legal effects is recognize as a unilateral act of state. For example, in the formation process of an international customary rule, in case of beneficiary State silence, this silence will be meant as being content with the formation of such a rule. When a State makes itself committed to do something by an unequivocal manifestation, it declares usually the specific commitment unilaterally. Sometimes States show their policies toward some certain issues by the issuance of a declaration in which their viewpoint or redlines have been stipulated. Such declarations have the legal effect and, under certain circumstances, are binding for their creator, including, Ihlen[1], Egypt[2], Iran[3] and France[4] declarations. Declarations can be issued in both verbal and written forms, none of them has superiority over the other.

The plural decision of some countries with a single interest may lead to an agreement, which does not include a treaty and, rather, is a collective act including Allied declaration[5] and EEC[6]. The notice is a unilateral act in which a state accepts some specific facts about other states or organizations. Also there is another important kind of unilateral act of State which is the formal representatives of states body language which has this potential to create legal effects including, clapping, standing up, and shaking hands. The warm welcome of more than fifty member state representatives in the Ministerial Conference of OSCE in Maastricht for the new representative of Georgian government after the coup d'état could be equivalent to their recognition.

2.5.1. Guiding Principles Applicable to Unilateral Declarations of States Capable of Creating Legal Obligations, with Commentaries thereto 2006.

1. Declarations publicly made and manifesting the will to be bound may have the effect of creating legal obligations. When the conditions for this are met, the binding character of such declarations is based on good faith; States concerned may then take them into consideration and rely on them; such States are

---

1. That is the name of the foreign minister of Norway, *Nils Claus Ihlen* and include his declaration to the Danish minister.
2. The *Egypt declaration on Suez Canal*, on April 24, 1957.
3. The *nuclear Fatwa* issued by Iran's supreme leader, 2004.
4. France *nuclear testing case*, 1974.
5. Issued in 1945 about Germany.
6. European Economic Community.

entitled to require that such obligations be respected.

Commentary

(1) The wording of Guiding Principle 1, which seeks both to define unilateral acts in the strict sense and to indicate what they are based on, is very directly inspired by the dicta in the Judgments handed down by the International Court of Justice on 20 December 1974 in the Nuclear Tests case.[1] In the case concerning the Frontier Dispute (Burkina Faso v. Republic of Mali), the Court was careful to point out that "it all depends on the intention of the State in question".[2]

(2) Most of the cases studied illustrate this principle. Besides the declarations made by France in 1974 on the cessation of nuclear tests in the atmosphere, the public nature of the declaration made by Egypt on 24 April 1957 on the Suez Canal[3] and Jordan's waiver of claims to the West Bank territories[4] represent an important indication of their authors' intention to commit themselves. The Ihlen Declaration, made during a purely bilateral meeting between the Minister for Foreign Affairs of Denmark and the Norwegian ambassador to Copenhagen,[5] and the Colombian diplomatic note addressed solely to the Venezuelan authorities are not counter examples: they relate only to bilateral relations between the two

---

1. *Nuclear Tests (Australia v. France; New Zealand v. France)*, Judgments dated 20 December 1974, *I.C.J. Reports 1974*, pp. 267-8, paras. 43 and 46 and pp. 472-3, paras. 46 and 49.

2. *Case concerning the Frontier Dispute (Burkina Faso v. Republic of Mali)*, Judgment of 22 December 1986, *I.C.J. Reports 1986*, p. 573, para. 39.

3. Document A/CN.4/557, paras. 55-58; see also paras. 62 and 63.

4. *Ibid.*, paras. 44-45.

5. *Ibid.*, paras. 116-126; *Legal Status of Eastern Greenland*, Judgment of 5 April 1933, *P.C.I.J.*, Series A/B, No. 53, p. 71. It should, however, be pointed out that whether this declaration constituted a unilateral act is controversial (see A/CN.4/557, para. 122).

States concerned.[1]

On this basis that nuclear fatwa has been publicly made and obligate Islamic Republic of Iran to the specific commitments, has the legal binding aspect for Iranian State.

2. Any State possesses capacity to undertake legal obligations through unilateral declarations.

Commentary

Just as "(e)very State possesses capacity to conclude treaties"[2], every State can commit itself through acts whereby it unilaterally undertakes legal obligations under the conditions indicated in these Guiding Principles. This capacity has been acknowledged by the International Court of Justice.[3] Accordingly, Islamic Republic of Iran's capacity in presentation of nuclear fatwa is definitive and inviolable.

3. To determine the legal effects of such declarations, it is necessary to take account of their content, of all the factual circumstances in which they were made, and of the reactions to which they gave rise.

Commentary

(1) The wording of Guiding Principle 3 is also inspired by a passage in the ICJ Judgments in the Nuclear Tests cases;[4] allusion is made to this jurisprudence in the Judgments of 22 December 1986 in the Frontier Dispute (Burkina Faso v. Republic of Mali) case[5] and of 3 February 2006 in the Armed Activities on the

---

1. See Guiding Principle 6 below. Vienna Convention on the Law of Treaties, 23 May 1969, article 6.
2. Vienna Convention on the Law of Treaties, 23 May 1969, article 6.
3. See the jurisprudence cited in support of Guiding Principles 1 and 3.
4. *Nuclear Tests (Australia v. France; New Zealand v. France), I.C.J. Reports 1974*, pp. 269-70, para. 51, and pp. 474-5, para. 53.
5. *Case concerning the Frontier Dispute (Burkina Faso v. Republic of*

Territory of the Congo case.[1] In the Military and Paramilitary Activities in and against Nicaragua and Frontier Dispute cases, the Court found nothing in the content of the declarations cited or the circumstances in which they were made "from which it [could] be inferred that any legal undertaking was intended to exist".[2]

(2) Generally speaking, the cases studied by the Commission confirm the relevance of this principle. In the Commission's view, it is particularly important to take account of the context and circumstances in which the declarations were made in the case of the Swiss statements concerning the privileges and immunities of United Nations staff,[3] the Egyptian declaration of 1957[4] and Jordan's waiver of claims to the West Bank territories.[5]

(3) Several of these examples show the importance of the reactions of other States concerned in evaluating the legal scope of the

---

Mali), I.C.J. Reports 1986, pp. 573-4, paras. 39-40

1. *Case concerning Armed Activities on the Territory of the Congo (New Application: 2002) (Democratic Republic of the Congo v. Rwanda), Jurisdiction of the Court and Admissibility of the Application*, para. 49.

2. *Case concerning Military and Paramilitary Activities in and against Nicaragua (Nicaragua v. United States of America)*, Judgment of 27 June 1986, *I.C.J. Reports 1986*, p. 132, para. 261, and *Case concerning the Frontier Dispute (Burkina Faso v. Republic of Mali), I.C.J. Reports 1986*, p. 573, para. 39.

3. A/CN.4/557, para. 157.

4. *Ibid.*, paras. 58-60 or 66. See also, by analogy, in the case of conduct other than unilateral statements, the
courses of conduct followed by Thailand and Cambodia in the *Temple of Preah Vihear* case (*ibid.*, paras. 160-167
and *Case concerning the Temple of Preah Vihea (Cambodia v. Thailand)* Judgment of 15 June 1962, *I.C.J. Reports
1962*, pp. 32-34).

5. *Ibid.*, paras. 47-48. **937** Cf. the international community's reactions to the Egyptian statement on the Suez Canal (*ibid.*, paras. 63-64);
also the reactions to Jordan's statement about the West Bank (*ibid.*, paras. 48 and 50-51).

unilateral acts in question, whether those States take cognizance of commitments undertaken[1] (or, in some cases, rights asserted[2]), or, on the contrary, object to[3] or challenge the binding nature of the "commitments" at issue.[4]

Nuclear fatwa is rooted in the profound Islamic teachings and as well the fundamental principles of human rights. For this reason, is respectable for international community and has received positive feedbacks[5].

4. A unilateral declaration binds the State internationally only if it is made by an authority vested with the power to do so. By virtue of their functions, heads of State, heads of Government and ministers for foreign affairs are competent to formulate such declarations. Other persons representing the State in specified areas may be authorized to bind it, through their declarations, in areas falling within their competence.

---

1. Cf. the international community's reactions to the Egyptian statement on the Suez Canal (*ibid.*, paras. 63-64); also the reactions to Jordan's statement about the West Bank (*ibid.*, paras. 48 and 50-51).
2. Cf. the reactions of certain States to the Truman Proclamation (*ibid.*, paras. 132-134); also the note dated 22 November 1952 by the Venezuelan Government concerning the Los Monjes archipelago (*ibid.*, para. 17 - yet like the Ihlen Declaration (see footnote 926 above) this note was clearly a matter of bilateral negotiations with Colombia).
3. See in particular Uruguay's refusal of a donation of vaccines from Cuba (*ibid.*, paras. 38-39) or the Russian
protest at the law passed by Turkmenistan in 1993 on the delimitation of its internal and territorial waters in the
Caspian Sea (*ibid.*, paras. 84-98).
4. Cf. the reactions of the non-nuclear-weapon States to the statements made in April 1995 to the Conference on
Disarmament by the permanent members of the Security Council (*ibid.*, paras. 113-115); their scepticism is,
incidentally, vindicated by the content of those statements.
5. Please see the pictures.

Commentary

(1) Guiding Principle 4 is also inspired by the consistent jurisprudence of the P.C.I.J. and I.C.J., on unilateral acts and the capacity of State authorities to represent and commit the State internationally. In its recent Judgment on jurisdiction and admissibility in the case of Armed Activities on the Territory of the Congo, the International Court of Justice observed, referring to the similar customary rule in the law of treaties,[1] that "in accordance with its consistent jurisprudence (Nuclear Tests (Australia v. France), Judgment, I.C.J. Reports 1974, pp. 269-270, paras. 49-51; Application of the Convention on the Prevention and Punishment of the Crime of Genocide (Bosnia and Herzegovina v. Yugoslavia), Preliminary Objections, Judgment, I.C.J. Reports 1996 (II), p. 622, para. 44; Arrest Warrant of 11 April 2000 (Democratic Republic of the Congo v. Belgium), Judgment, I.C.J. Reports 2002, pp. 21-22, para. 53; see also Legal Status of Eastern Greenland (Denmark v. Norway), Judgment, 1933, P.C.I.J., Series A/B, No. 53, p. 71), it is a well-established rule of international law that the Head of State, the Head of Government and the Minister for Foreign Affairs are deemed to represent the State merely by virtue of exercising their functions, including for the performance, on behalf of the said State of unilateral acts having the force of international commitments".[2]

(2) State practice shows that unilateral declarations creating legal obligations for States are quite often made by heads of State

---

1. Cf. article 7 of the 1969 Vienna Convention on the Law of Treaties.
2. *Case concerning Armed Activities on the Territory of the Congo (New Application: 2002) (Democratic Republic of the Congo v. Rwanda)*, Judgment of 3 February 2006, *Jurisdiction of the Court and Admissibility of the Application*, para. 46.

or Government[1] or ministers for foreign affairs[2] without their capacity to commit the State being called into question. In the two examined cases in which problems relating to the extent of the speaker's authority arose both related to compliance with the domestic law of the State concerned.[3] The statement by the King of Jordan relating to the West Bank, which some considered to be ultra vires under the Constitution of the Kingdom, was confirmed by subsequent domestic acts.[4] In the case of the declaration by the Colombian Minister for Foreign Affairs about Venezuelan sovereignty over the Los Monjes archipelago, the note itself was set aside in domestic law because its author had no authority to make such a commitment, yet the Colombian authorities did not challenge the validity of the commitment at the international

---

1. See the statement made on 31 July 1988 by the King of Jordan waiving Jordan's claims to the West Bank territories (A/CN.4/557, para. 44), the Egyptian declaration of 24 April 1957 on the Suez Canal, made by the Egyptian Government (*ibid.*, para. 55), the statements of 8 June and 25 July 1974 and the letter of 1 July 1974 by the President of the French Republic (*ibid.*, para. 71) or the statement made on 28 September 1945 by President Truman of the United States concerning the continental shelf (*ibid.*, para. 127).

2. See the note dated 22 November 1952 from the Colombian Minister for Foreign Affairs relating to Venezuelan sovereignty over the Los Monjes archipelago (*ibid.*, para. 13), the statement from the Minister for Foreign Affairs of Cuba about the supply of vaccines to Uruguay (*ibid.*, para. 36), the statement by the French Minister for Foreign Affairs to the United Nations General Assembly on 25 September 1974 about the cessation of nuclear tests in the atmosphere (*ibid.*, para. 71), the statements made, as representatives of nuclear-weapon States, by the Minister for Foreign Affairs of the Russian Federation and the United States Secretary of State to the United Nations Security Council (*ibid.*, para. 106), and the statement by Mr. Ihlen, the Minister for Foreign Affairs of Norway (*ibid.*, para. 116).

3. See the case of the statement made by the Colombian Minister for Foreign Affairs on 22 November 1952 (*ibid.*, paras. 24-35) and the statement by the King of Jordan about the West Bank (*ibid.*, paras. 53-54).

4. *Ibid.*, para. 54.

level.[1]

(3) In its Judgment of 3 February 2006,[2] the I.C.J., did, however, note that "with increasing frequency in modern international relations other persons representing a State in specific fields may be authorized by that State to bind it by their statements in respect of matters falling within their purview. This may be true, for example, of holders of technical ministerial portfolios exercising powers in their field of competence in the area of foreign relations, and even of certain officials".[3] Based on the principles set forth in Islamic Republic of Iran's Constitution, Valiyeh-Faqih has the highest official position in the sovereignty and is vested with power to issue such a binding statements.

5. Unilateral declarations may be formulated orally or in writing.

Commentary

(1) It is generally accepted that the form of a unilateral declaration does not affect its validity or legal effects. The I.C.J. mentioned the relative unimportance of formalities[4] in its Judgment in the Temple of Preah Vihear case in connection with unilateral conduct.[5] In the Nuclear Tests cases, the Court emphasized that "[w]ith regard to the question of form, it should be observed that

---

1. *Ibid.*, para. 35.
2. *Case concerning Armed Activities on the Territory of the Congo (New Application: 2002) (Democratic Republic of the Congo v. Rwanda), Jurisdiction of the Court and Admissibility of the Application*, para. 46.
3. *Ibid.*, para. 47.
4. See *The Mavrommatis Palestine Concessions*, Judgment of 30 August 1924, P.C.I..J,. Series A, No. 2, p. 34; *Application of the Convention on the Prevention and Punishment of the Crime of Genocide (Bosnia-Herzegovina v. Yugoslavia)*, Judgment of 11 July 1996, *I.C.J. Reports 1996*, p. 612, para. 24 and p. 613, para. 26.
5. *Case concerning the Temple of Preah Vihear (Cambodia v. Thailand), Preliminary Objections*, Judgment of 26 May 1961, *I.C.J. Reports 1961*, p. 31.

this is not a domain in which international law imposes any special or strict requirements. Whether a statement is made orally or in writing makes no essential difference, for such statements made in particular circumstances may create commitments in international law, which does not require that they should be couched in written form. Thus the question of form is not decisive".[1]

(2) State practice also shows the many different forms that unilateral declarations by States may take. The various declarations by France about the cessation of atmospheric nuclear tests took the form of a communiqué from the Office of the President of the Republic, a diplomatic note, a letter from the President of the Republic sent directly to those to whom the declaration was addressed, a statement made during a press conference and a speech to the General Assembly.[2] Other examples also go to show that, while written declarations prevail,[3] it is not unusual for States to commit themselves by simple oral statements.[4]

(3) France's statements on the suspension of atmospheric nuclear tests also show that a unilateral commitment by a State can come

---

1. *Nuclear Tests (Australia v. France; New Zealand v. France), I.C.J. Reports 1974*, pp. 267-268, para. 45, and p. 473, para. 48.
2. Cf. Eighth report, A/CN.4/557, paras. 71 and 72.
3. Consider the examples of the note dated 22 November 1952 from the Colombian Minister for Foreign Affairs (*ibid.*, para. 13), the Egyptian declaration of 24 April 1957 (*ibid.*, paras. 55 ff.), the protests by the Russian Federation against Turkmenistan and Azerbaijan (*ibid.*, paras. 85 and 99), the statements by the nuclear-weapon States (statements made before an international body, *ibid.*, paras. 106-107), the Truman Proclamation of 28 September 1945 (*ibid.*, para. 127) and the Swiss statements concerning the United Nations and its staff members (tax exemptions and privileges) (*ibid.*, paras. 140-142).
4. See, for example, Jordan's waiver of its claims to the West Bank territories in a public speech, (*ibid.*, para. 44) or the Ihlen Declaration (*ibid.*, para. 117 - see *Legal Status of Eastern Greenland*, Judgment of 5 April 1933, *P.C.I.J., Series A./B.*, No. 53, p. 71.

about through a series of declarations with the same general thrust, none of which might, in isolation, have bound the State. In its Judgments of 1974 on the Nuclear Tests cases, the I.C.J. did not concentrate on any particular declaration by the French authorities but took them, together, to constitute a whole: "[the] statements [by the President of the French Republic], and those of members of the French Government acting under his authority, up to the last statement made by the Minister of Defense (of 11 October 1974), constitute a whole. Thus, in whatever form the statements were expressed, they must be held to constitute an engagement of the State, having regard to their intention and to the circumstances in which they were made".[1] In this respect, both verbal and written form of nuclear fatwa is confirmed and available.

6. Unilateral declarations may be addressed to the international community as a whole, to one or several States or to other entities.

Commentary

(1) Several of the cases examined remain within the scope of strictly bilateral relations between two States; accordingly these unilateral declarations by a State had another State as the sole addressee. Such was the case of the Colombian diplomatic note addressed to Venezuela,[2] the Cuban declarations concerning the supply of vaccines to Uruguay,[3] the protests by the Russian Federation against Turkmenistan and Azerbaijan[4] and the Ihlen Declaration.[5]

---

1. *Nuclear Tests (Australia v. France; New Zealand v. France), I.C.J. Reports 1974*, p. 269, para. 49, and p. 474, para. 51. See also the Swiss statements concerning the United Nations and its staff members (tax exemptions and privileges) A/CN.4/557, paras. 138-156).
2. A/CN.4/557, paras. 15 and 16.
3. *Ibid.*, para. 36.
4. *Ibid.*, paras. 85 and 99.
5. *Ibid.*, para. 117.

(2) Although initially concerning a limited group of States, other declarations were addressed to the international community as a whole, containing erga omnes undertakings. Thus, Egypt's declaration regarding the Suez Canal was not addressed only to the States parties to the Constantinople Convention or to the States members of the Suez Canal Users' Association, but to the entire international community.[1] Similarly, the Truman Proclamation,[2] and also the French declarations regarding suspension of nuclear tests in the atmosphere, although the latter were of more direct concern to Australia and New Zealand, as well as certain neighboring States[3] were also made erga omnes and, accordingly, were addressed to the international community in its entirety.[4] The same holds for the declaration by the King of Jordan of 31 July 1988, waiving Jordan's claims to the West Bank territories, which was addressed simultaneously to the international community, to another State (Israel) and to another entity the Palestine Liberation Organization (PLO).[5] The audience of nuclear fatwa is the biggest target society, i.e. international community at all times[6].

7. A unilateral declaration entails obligations for the formulating State only if it is stated in clear and specific terms. In the case of

---

1. *Ibid.*, para. 62.
2. *Ibid.*, para. 127.
3. Fiji filed an application to intervene in the proceedings. The Government of Argentina, Fiji and Peru requested that the pleadings and annexed documents should be made available to them. See *Nuclear Tests (Australia v. France; New Zealand v. France), I.C.J. Reports 1974*, p. 6, paras. 7 and 9.
4. *Ibid.*, p. 269, paras. 50 and 51 and p. 474, paras. 52 and 53.
5. A/CN.4/557, para. 45. Other unilateral declarations are addressed to one or more international organizations, as is the case with Switzerland's declarations concerning the United Nations and its staff (tax exemptions and privileges) (*ibid.*, paras. 138 et seq.).
6. There is no any word in text of fatwa to limit it to a specific time or place in terms of his addressees.

doubt as to the scope of the obligations resulting from such a declaration, such obligations must be interpreted in a restrictive manner. In interpreting the content of such obligations, weight shall be given first and foremost to the text of the declaration, together with the context and the circumstances in which it was formulated.

Commentary

(1) In its Judgments in the Nuclear Tests cases, the International Court of Justice stressed that a unilateral declaration may have the effect of creating legal obligations for the State making the declaration only if it is stated in clear and specific terms.[1] This understanding has been adopted without change by the Court in the case concerning Armed Activities on the Territory of the Congo.[2]

(2) In case of doubt concerning the legal scope of the unilateral declaration, it must be interpreted in a restrictive manner, as clearly stated by the Court in its Judgments in the Nuclear Tests cases when it held that, "when States make statements by which their freedom of action is to be limited, a restrictive interpretation is called for".[3] The interpreter must therefore proceed with great caution in determining the legal effects of unilateral declarations, in particular when the unilateral declaration has no specific addressee.[4]

---

1. *Nuclear Tests (Australia v. France; New Zealand v. France), I.C.J. Reports 1974*, p. 267, para. 43, p. 269, para. 51, and p. 472, para. 46, p. 474, para. 53.

2. *Armed Activities on the Territory of the Congo (New application: 2002) (Democratic Republic of the Congo v. Rwanda), Jurisdiction and Admissibility*, paras. 50 and 52.

3. *Nuclear Tests (Australia v. France; New Zealand v. France), I.C.J. Reports 1974*, p. 267, para. 44, and pp. 472 and 473, para. 47.

4. *Frontier Dispute (Burkina Faso v. Republic of Mali), I.C.J. Reports 1986*, p. 574, para. 39.

(3) With regard, in particular, to the method and means of the interpretation, attention is drawn to the observation by the International Court of Justice that "[t]he régime relating to the interpretation of declarations made under Article 36 of the Statute [¹] is not identical with that established for the interpretation of treaties by the Vienna Convention on the Law of Treaties (...). Spain has suggested in its pleadings that '[t]his does not mean that the legal rules and the art of interpreting declarations (and reservations) do not coincide with those governing the interpretation of treaties'. The Court observes that the provisions of that Convention may only apply analogously to the extent compatible with the sui generis character of the unilateral acceptance of the Court's jurisdiction".[2] Applying the Court's dictum and by analogy with article 31, paragraph 1, of the 1969 Vienna Convention on the Law of Treaties, priority consideration must be given to the text of the unilateral declaration, which best reflects its author's intentions. In addition, as acknowledged by the Court in its Judgment in the Frontier Dispute case, "to assess the intentions of the author of a unilateral act, account must be taken of all the circumstances in which the act occurred",[3] which

---

1. Declarations accepting the compulsory jurisdiction of the International Court of Justice made under Article 36 of the Statute of the Court lie outside the scope of the present study (see above, footnote 1). That said, the Court's reasoning is fully applicable to unilateral acts and declarations *stricto sensu*.

2. *Fisheries Jurisdiction (Spain v. Canada), Merits*, Judgment of 4 December 1998, *I.C.J. Reports 1998*, p. 453, para. 46. See also *Land and Maritime Boundary between Cameroon and Nigeria (Cameroon v. Nigeria), Preliminary Objections*, Judgment of 11 June 1998, *I.C.J. Reports 1998*, p. 293, para. 30.

3. *Frontier Dispute (Burkina Faso v. Republic of Mali), I.C.J. Reports 1986*, p. 574, para. 40; see also *Armed Activities on the Territory of the Congo (New Application: 2002) (Democratic Republic of the Congo v. Rwanda), Jurisdiction and Admissibility*, para. 53, and *Nuclear Tests*

constitutes an application by analogy of article 31, paragraph 2, of the 1969 Vienna Convention. On this basis the scope of nuclear fatwa's commitment is in clear and specific terms and any probability of the vagueness is impossible.

8. A unilateral declaration which is in conflict with a peremptory norm of general international law is void.

Commentary

The invalidity of a unilateral act which is contrary to a peremptory norm of international law derives from the analogous rule contained in article 53 of the 1969 Vienna Convention on the Law of Treaties. Most members of the Commission agreed that there was no obstacle to the application of this rule to the case of unilateral declarations.[1] In its Judgment in the Armed Activities on the Territory of the Congo case, the Court did not exclude the possibility that a unilateral declaration by Rwanda[2] could be invalid in the event that it was in conflict with a norm of jus cogens, which proved, however, not to be the case.[3] Nuclear fatwa not only is not in conflict with international peremptory norms but also there is a total affinity between them.

9. No obligation may result for other States from the unilateral declaration of a State. However, the other State or States concerned may incur obligations in relation to such a unilateral declaration to

(Australia v. France; New Zealand v. France), I.C.J. Reports 1974, p. 269, para. 51, and p. 474, para. 53.

1. *Official Records of the General Assembly, Fifty-fourth Session, Supplement No. 10* (A/54/10), p. 332, para. 557; *ibid., Fifty-fifth Session, Supplement No. 10* (A/55/10), p. 203, para. 597.

2. The declaration in this case was a reservation, a unilateral act which lies outside the scope of the present Guiding Principles (see paragraph 174 above).

3. *Armed Activities on the Territory of the Congo (New Application: 2002) (Democratic Republic of the Congo v. Rwanda), Jurisdiction and Admissibility*, para. 69.

the extent that they clearly accepted such a declaration.

Commentary

(1) It is well established in international law that obligations cannot be imposed by a State upon another State without its consent. For the law of treaties, this principle has been codified in article 34 of the 1969 Vienna Convention.[1] There is no reason why this principle should not also apply to unilateral declarations; the consequence is that a State cannot impose obligations on other States to which it has addressed a unilateral declaration unless the latter unequivocally accept these obligations resulting from that declaration.[2] In the circumstances, the State or States concerned are in fact bound by their own acceptance.

(2) The 1945 Truman Proclamation, by which the United States of America aimed to impose obligations on other States or, at least, to limit their rights on the American continental shelf, was not strictly speaking accepted by other States. All the same, as the Court has stressed, "this régime [of the continental shelf] furnishes an example of a legal theory derived from a particular source that has secured a general following".[3] In fact, the other States responded to the Truman Proclamation with analogous claims and declarations[4] and, shortly thereafter, the content of

---

1. This article states: "A treaty does not create either obligations or rights for a third State without its consent." See also *Reservations to the Convention on the Prevention and Punishment of the Crime of Genocide, I.C.J. Reports 1951*, p. 21.

2. Or if there was a general norm authorizing States to take such action; but the unilateral acts made pursuant to a norm of this kind lie outside the scope of the present Guiding Principles (see paragraph 174 above).

3. *North Sea Continental Shelf (Federal Republic of Germany v. Denmark; Federal Republic of Germany v. Netherlands), I.C.J Reports 1969*, p. 53, para. 100.

4. See the case of Mexico, A/CN.4/557, para. 132.

the Proclamation was taken up in article 2 of the 1958 Geneva Convention on the Continental Shelf. It could therefore be said to have been generally accepted and it marked a point of departure for a customary process leading, in a very short time, to a new norm of international law. The International Court of Justice remarked in that context: "The Truman Proclamation however, soon came to be regarded as a starting point of the positive law on the subject, and the chief doctrine it enunciated ... came to prevail over all others, being now reflected in article 2 of the 1958 Geneva Convention on the Continental Shelf."[1] In this context, with regard to authenticity of verbal and non-verbal behaviour of state authorities, confirmation of legal regime of nuclear fatwa and acknowledgement of its justice- based approach can make an unwritten commitment in road of custom-making process of nuclear fatwa.

10. A unilateral declaration that has created legal obligations for the State making the declaration cannot be revoked arbitrarily. In assessing whether a revocation would be arbitrary, consideration should be given to:

(a) Any specific terms of the declaration relating to revocation;

(b) The extent to which those to whom the obligations are owed have relied on such obligations;

(c) The extent to which there has been a fundamental change in the circumstances.

Commentary

(1) In its 1974 Judgments in the Nuclear Tests cases, the International Court of Justice states that "the unilateral undertaking resulting from [the French] statements cannot be

---

1. *North Sea Continental Shelf (Federal Republic of Germany v. Denmark; Federal Republic of Germany v. Netherlands)*, I.C.J Reports 1969, para. 47.

interpreted as having been made in implicit reliance on an arbitrary power of reconsideration".[1] This does not, however, exclude any power to terminate a unilateral act, only its arbitrary withdrawal (or amendment).

(2) There can be no doubt that unilateral acts may be withdrawn or amended in certain specific circumstances. The Commission has drawn up an open-ended list of criteria to be taken into consideration when determining whether or not a withdrawal is arbitrary.

(3) A similar case obtains where the declaration itself stipulates the circumstances in which its author may terminate it[2] or when its addressees have relied on it in good faith and have accordingly been led "detrimentally to change position or suffer some prejudice".[3] A unilateral declaration may also be rescinded following a fundamental change of circumstances within the meaning and within the strict limits of the customary rule enshrined in article 62 of the 1969 Vienna Convention on the Law of Treaties.[4] With regard to the nature of nuclear fatwa that is primary governmental decree under Islamic jurisprudence and Iranian constitution, the probability of its change or revocation is permanently impossible[5]

---

1. *Nuclear Tests (Australia v. France; New Zealand v. France), I.C.J. Reports 1974*, p. 270, para. 51, and p. 475, para. 53.
2. *When the condition of the circumstances do not exist.*
3. *Military and Paramilitary Activities in and against Nicaragua (Nicaragua v. United States of America), Jurisdiction of the Court and Admissibility of the Application, I.C.J. Reports 1984*, p. 415, para. 51.
4. *Fisheries jurisdiction (Germany v. Iceland), Jurisdiction of the Court, I.C.J. Reports 1973*, p. 63, para. 36, and *Case concerning the Gabcikovo-Nagymaros Project (Hungary v. Slovakia), I.C.J. Reports 1997*, p. 64, para. 104.
5. In this part, referring to issuance of Imam khomeini's fatwa in prohibition of chemical weapons during imposed war against Iran is very important point to be considered, especially in proving the inviolability of primary

state order. Non utilization of chemical weapons was not because of Iran's disability in achieving to formula of chemical combination, rather because Imam Khomeini had banned these weapons under Islamic jurisprudence. According to Pro. Mousavian (Senior officials of the Ministry of Foreign Affairs), when Saddam utilized chemical weapons against Iran, by resorting to the principle of retaliation some of Iranian official authorities tried to persuade the leaders to retaliate in kind against Saddam, but they encounter a big ban which was embodied in Imam Khomeini's fatwa concerning the prohibition of chemical armaments use.(Mousavian, 2010, p13) Iran needed a relative prevention in front of Saddam's chemical attacks, that is why this fatwa never publicized during the imposed war against Iran.

Chapter Three

Formation of an International Custom Based on the Legal Regime of the Nuclear Fatwa and its Comparative Study with Non Proliferation Treaty and Advisory Opinion of International Court of Justice

3.1. Generalities

The legal regime of the nuclear fatwa, according to the features emanating from the principles of justice and security, is offering a new approach in the system of disarmament and non-proliferation of the weapons of mass destruction. The growing international acceptance of this approach and the fluid nature of the boundaries of the international law development, especially in the realm of customary international law on the one hand, and the ineffectiveness of the related treaty and mechanisms on the other, underlies the genesis of a new custom emanating from the legal regime of the nuclear Fatwa[1]. This fact requires the necessity of taking advantage of studies in the field of religion and religious beliefs, particularly in religious States and communities. And more pronounced that, the purpose of the international law and monotheistic religions is placed in one direction. This means that,

---

1. In this respect various efforts, in primary formation of an international custom emanating from the mentioned legal regime can be stated such as; hold of international conference on disarmament in Tehran, bilateral and multilateral meetings with international high level authorities on clarifying IRI's peaceful approach and idea, the globally idea of the formation of an international convention on investigation of nuclear threats after the issuance of nuclear fatwa, registration of nuclear fatwa as an internationally legal act in United Nations and support of the noted Christian, Jewish religious figures from the issuance of nuclear fatwa and many other relevant cases.

if we want to consider a common denominator between them, that would be the maintenance of global[1] peace and security, the only difference is in a word, and that is justice, i.e. maintaining international peace and security in terms of justice. Therefore, in the message that Iran's supreme leader sent in response to president Obama[2], he noted this fact, and president also, in his speech in Berlin, uttered this sentence that international peace and security is realizable only in terms of justice. And asserted that if this matter is realized, there will not be any need to war in the world. It is evident that the function of the religious values, as the most universal values, has a specific capacity that can be very effective in the genesis of modern international law, as most of the customary rules shaped based on the values root in religious beliefs. Thus, it can be said that the values derived from religion and monotheistic thoughts, beside influencing the creations of international customs, have had a constructive role in sources genesis of the international law, such as the general principles of law or peremptory norms of international law such as: the principle of fulfilment of the obligation, good will, non-violence, non-aggression, prohibition of Genocide, prohibition of crimes against humanity, prohibition of war crimes, non-racial discrimination, non-polluting the environment, respect for fundamental human rights and etc. What is evident is that in the formation of the international custom, how far we proceed in the twentieth century, the position of persons gets stronger, in comparison with States that once were the main functions of the international law, and this change of direction in the process of formation and recognition of the international law is very important. This can be viewed from two perspectives: first, Ayatollah Khamenei's Fatwa, as a person, and in the framework of individual system, lead to the development of

---

1. Peace and security with international peculiarity has the lowest level toward global security, because it may merely include two countries.

2. That is available on: http://www.dw.de/a-16894996

the international customary law and second, as the governmental practice of IRI leads to the development of international law. Even though there are some special international bi or multilateral acts[1] in the prohibition of WMD, but none of them could have made a general prohibition which, in the light of a unit system proscribes any access, production, stockpiling and use of "all sorts of" weapons of mass destruction. The nuclear fatwa, accordingly, has this potential to be a precursor to the formation of such a process.

The nuclear fatwa's custom-building in several phases of this process can be studied; firstly, it can only be the customization of the nuclear Fatwa. Secondly, the custom making its content and

---

1. Hague convention on prohibition of poisonous gases (1907), Convention on the prohibition of the development, production, stockpiling and use of chemical weapons and on their destruction, Paris (1993), Convention on the Prohibition of the Development, Production and Stockpiling of Bacteriological (Biological) and Toxin Weapons and on their Destruction or Biological and Toxin Weapons Convention (BTWC) (1972), In ICC Statute has been considered as a war crime, Comprehensive Nuclear-Test-Ban Treaty (CTBT), Geneva Protocol, Brussels Convention on the Law and Customs of War, Strasbourg Agreement, Treaty of Versailles, Washington Naval Treaty, Seabed Arms Control Treaty, Outer Space Treaty, Statute of the International Atomic Energy Agency, Convention on the Physical Protection of Nuclear Material, African Nuclear-Weapon-Free Zone Treaty, Antarctic Treaty, Central Asian Nuclear Weapon Free Zone, Treaty on the Final Settlement with Respect to Germany, Treaty for the Prohibition of Nuclear Weapons in Latin America and the Caribbean, South Atlantic Peace and Cooperation Zone, South Pacific Nuclear Free Zone Treaty, Southeast Asian Nuclear-Weapon-Free Zone Treaty, India–United States Civil Nuclear Agreement, Fissile Material Cut-off Treaty (not completed), Intermediate-Range Nuclear Forces Treaty, McCloy–Zorin Accords Partial Nuclear Test Ban Treaty, SALT I (Strategic Arms Limitation Talks), SALT II, Strategic Offensive Reductions Treaty (SORT), START I (Strategic Arms Reduction Treaty), START II, START III (not completed), New START (2010), 1958 US–UK Mutual Defense Agreement, Nassau Agreement, Polaris Sales Agreement, Quebec Agreement (with Canada).

what is reflected by Fatwa and thirdly, subtraction for the formation of other emerging customs; in other words, our point, when we say what the relationship between the international custom and this Fatwa is, not only this fatwa becomes or has become a customary rule, but non usage of WMD based on general principles of law and other sources of the international law has been accepted as a customary practice under the international law and this Fatwa, in this regard is effective in the formation and consolidation in both material fact and opinio juris elements, and at the another level, it can be argued in this way whether the Fatwas issued by *Valliye-Faqih* that have the same international features can cause the formation of a regional custom or not? Specifically with regard to the Islamic nature of middle-east area.

Nowadays there are so many discussions about the moral war under the international law, that must be considered whether Iran's supreme leader' edict could take a positive step in this respect or not? And also, has it been effective in the formation of the moral war custom or not? Generally, there is no any treaty not to be in the road of custom making, all treaties and all unilateral acts are effective in this process, one less one more.(Seivanizad,2013) In this chapter, first we pay attention to the governing rules on the formation of the custom from the perspective of the international law, several approaches related to the formation of the custom including: traditional, modern and postmodern and, at the same time, we try to recognize and compare these ingredients with contents of the legal regime of nuclear fatwa and finally, to determine the limits of it.

3.2. Definition of International Custom:

Custom in the first step, is one action or omission of a joint action among countries and, in some cases, among international organizations, the meaning that it is resulted from the repetition of a legal documented action in a notable period. This characteristic is named material element. Custom in the second step displays as obligatory legal approach that this characteristic is named immaterial element.

3.3. Material Element:

Already, the definition of custom has been discussed in the international law. Regardless of theoretical disputes about Statute Article 38 (1) (B) international Court of justice, this concept consisted of two material (practice) and immaterial (legal belief) elements that the combination of them will lead to causing a legal rule (custom) at the international society level. These elements will be considered in detail in the following that the first material element will be viewed.

Generally, material element at the first step implies governments practice. As it mentioned, there are no written and specific rules about what qualifications the practice should have. Issues including length at which the practice should be considered, repetition of the practice, degree of the practice coherency and integrity, generality of the practice, essence of the practice and practices that are criteria in this framework and finally other makers of the practice other than governments are a part of most important issues that should be noticed in determination of this material element. Without any doubt, lawyers' ideas regarding international juridical practice are considered as a very valuable reservoir to achieve applicable standards for realizing custom material element. Mentioned issues without any priority on terms of writing will be discussed in detail as follows.

3.3.1. The Practice Makers,

3.3.1.1. States:

(general practice) that is accepted as law, inserted in 38 (1) (B) Article of international court of Justice Statute, basically indicates State practices and this issue is inferred from Court views well. States do not have physical entity. They are a collection of connected governing institutions (organs) that have a complete legal personality. Sovereignty is considered as constitution and the main emblem of government due to international law and is explanatory of its place in international relations.

In Max Hober's view in judgement related to Palmas island (1928); (sovereignty indicates the independence in relations between States.[1]) And independence also as has been put by Anzilotti at his personal theory in advisory view of international Permanent Court of justice in 1931 regarding tariff regimes between Austria and Germany, means that the State which according to international law has sovereignty, receives its entity and authority from that same international law[2]. State practices through qualified organs appear that form the main movement of rulemaking at international level. Determination of State qualified organs according to international law has been allotted to its own inside legal system. According to Article 4 of International law commission plan draft regarding international responsibility of states 2001, behavior of each governmental organ due to international law is considered as the practice of that government regardless of that organ has a decorative, legal, executive function or another function and whether what position the mentioned organ has in governmental organization and this organ is an element of central government or an element of local governmental unit (paragraph 1)[3].

---

1. Island of Palmas case (Netherlands/United States of America), 1928, Reports of International Arbitral Awards, p.829, 838.

2. Advisory Opinion on Customs Regime between Austria Germany, PCIJ, 1931, series AB, Individual Opinion of Judge Anzilotti, p.57.

3. The Draft Articles on Responsibility of States for International Wrongful

The way of separation of power and competency domain among government different organs also has been allotted to their inner system that of course following considerations should be considered: 1)although the determination of competency domain of formal organs is the responsibility of governments inner system, international law regarding some senior governmental authorities (e.g. the head of the state) considers them among government ostensible representative who even have competency behind what is defined in domestic system framework for them. Concerning making agreement, such a situation has been affirmed by international Court of justice in the case related to maritime and territorial boundary between Cameroon and Nigeria in 2002. And Court about this case has based its own verdict on Article 7 (2) of Wien convention on law of treaty 1969[1]. There is no reason to conceive that substantial difference exists in the relation between treaty-making and the process of custom-making (Danilenko, 1995). Nevertheless, we emphasize that the form of exerting such a verdict will include just some of state senior formal authorities.

2) When a government formal ordinary organ acts over its authorities, their behavior will not be contributed in the process of custom-making, albeit by doing a violating act, this issue ascribed to the State and consequently will followed by its international responsibility[2]. In other words, behavior outside authority domain of state formal organs – other than about a few number of senior authorities that already was mentioned – cannot be noticed as making element in rule making process, although it is possible - if being violating- to lead to the responsibility of states at international level(Danilenko,

---

Acts, United Nations, International Law Commission, 2001, fifty-third sessions, Article 4(1) (2).
1. Case concerning the Land of Maitimes Boundary between Cameron and Nigeria, ICJ Reports, 2002, p.430.
2. The Draft Articles on Responsibility of States for International Wrongful Acts, op.cit., Article7.

1998).

Concerning this issue, it needs to be stated that the executive power measures must be considered and not only foreign ministry. Leading of international negotiations and occasions in nowadays modern method is not always the responsibility of foreign ministry. This task can be done by economy, transportation ministry and etc. Other than the cases that an executive organ take measures outside its authority domain and its action is rejected by senior authority, apparently there are no appropriate reasons regarding that why state capacity of practice-creating be confined to foreign ministry[1]. ICJ in the case of the NotteBohmm 1955 states that a governmental rule (whether constitution that is possible, for example, to include claim of competency on maritime areas) can be considered as the manifestation of that state practice[2]. Court in Lutos verdict also emphasizes on this issue in the same manner that inner courts are part of government organs and their decisions must considered as a part of state practice[3]. Legislation of territorial rules and reflex ion of them in judicial verdicts during legal procedure can be viewed as notable indicatives of government behavior; particularly, basic and main rules of each country regarding limitation or development of government competencies, separation and resignation of authorities and promotion of human rights.

Also, verdicts issued from inner courts particularly can be suitable delineation of executive condition of legal processes, realization of justice immunities and extradition. In many case we see the state practice-making through association of the triple

---

1. Statement of Principles Applicable to The Formation of General Customary International Law, The International Law Association, Final Report of 69td Conference, London, 2000, article 9(Commentary b).
2. Nottebohm Case, ICJ Reports, 1955, p.22.
3. Lutos Case, op. cit., pp. 23, 26, 28 -29.

powers with each other. For example, the request of extradition is made. In this case, approving or disapproving national rule, inner court decision and accomplishment or not doing extradition by executive government can be a manifestation of government real practice regarding the mentioned issue (Gilbert, 1998, p.78).

Also about the governments that have confederation or federal position like US and Switzerland, it primarily must be told that practices of each of their inner territorial units – that also do not have international independent personality- cannot be viewed as state practice, unless their practices are on behalf of central government and or approve and pass by them[1]. Thus, state practice, as it was described, has a determining role in creating rules of customary international law. Indeed, States as main subjects of international system and their behavior and approach as the basic element of rule-making in this domain, has the most important and dominant role in the area of (practice makers). As it was considered, act of State can be appeared in act of its entities and executive power entities are not only under power of president or prime minister but it can contain measures of a system as a whole. So it is obvious that issuance of nuclear fatwa by supreme leader is equal with act of executive power, because based on Iran constitution, the final decision maker in Iran is supreme leader and determination of general and strategic policies are under his authority[2]. At first hypothesis, the primary element of custom making - practice- is referred to act of Valiye Faqih in issuance of the concerned fatwas and acknowledgement of peaceful activities and emphasis on nuclear fatwa by representatives of international communities[3]. At second hypothesis the primary element of custom making

---

1. Statement of Principles Applicable to The Formation of General Customary International Law, op. cit., Article 8.
2. In this respect, it was explained in detail in previous chapters.
3. Please see the pictures.

relates to act of Iran in non-usage, proliferation and stockpiling of weapons of mass destruction. And at third hypothesis practice relates to prohibitive and consistent act of inclined States to assist with Iran in connection with weapons of mass destruction. But in continuation, studying the other factors of practice-making under international law and their role in process of custom-making of nuclear fatwa is necessary to be considered.

3.3.1.2. International Organizations:

albeit "general practice" as the material element of custom-making basically indicate State practice; however, international organizations that are created to organize disorder in international relations in generating systemic order has increasingly developed these days and actually is considered as an inseparable part of international life and plays roles in different areas. This increasingly development has been the outcome of extension of international relations particularly in twentieth century.

international organizations that first has just took step in international domains in limited areas and the framework of technical issues, presently has generalized own activities domain to most important international issues including legal, political and security issues. Thus, international organizations due to having subjective legal personality are considered one of the active subjects of international law and therein can be both producer of right and obligation, and its subject. Although organizations firstly take this own personality form State will, they with continuance in their activities act as an independent legal personality[1]. Nevertheless, international organizations practice

---

1. Amerasinghe, C, F, Principles of the Institutional Law of International Organization, Cambridge University Press, 1996.
Gross, L, Essays on International Law and Organization, Two Vols, Martinus Nijhoff, 1984.

also can be effective in practice-making process and codifying legal rules because the practice of all subjects of international system contributed in generating and creating legal rules.

generally, as international organizations have capacity of treaty-making in international legal area to implement their missions and achieve aims that has been made for their realization – that its borders has been defined in Wien convention on law of treaty among countries and international organizations and or international organization with each other on March 21, 1986[1]- as they also can participate in the formation process of general customary international law through the practice of their organs[2].

Such association is actually of main impacts and consequences of having independent international legal personality. Of course, we should note that the acceptance of legal personality for international organizations should not lead to this conclusion that State members of an organization do not have any independent practice in involved organization framework anymore, and what is efficient in deduction of customary rules is only the practice of the organization itself. International organizations privilege of independent legal personality of constitutive members will not have any conflict with obtaining independent practice of State members of the organization, because one State do not lose own entity and identity due to enrolling in an international organization, rather it assigns some of own competencies and authorities to the related organization to achieve a specific aim. As we will see in the following, international organization resolutions,

---

1. Vienna Convention on the Law of Treaties Between States and International Organizations or Between International Organizations, Official Records of the United Nations Conference on the Law of Treaties Between States and International Organizations or Between International Organizations, 1986.
2. Statement of Principles Applicable to The Formation of General Customary International Law, op. cit., Article 11.

particularly, United Nations General Assembly resolutions are a very appropriate place to assess State practices in discussed issues and a manifestation and reflective of their legal belief. International Court of Justice in advisory verdict related to the reservation on genocide Convention1951, in explanation of customary law related to reservation, noted the practice of United Nations Secretary General as trustee of many of multilateral treaties alongside the State practice of national authorities[1].

Regardless of the above case as an example of organization behavior, many of other practices of international organizations through their decisions appear in the form of responsible authorities' resolution, statement, and declarations. Therefore, presentation of such documents can be considered as a clear sample of organization practice. Concerning this, even some authors view organization approach as a custom constitutive material element as concrete only in this form and do not accept crystallization of the organization tangible function in the way described above (Higgins, R 1987, p.39) Oppositely, some others of commentators seek organization practice manifestation just in the framework of tangible behavior of it (and not verbal in the form of resolution and statement) (Mandelson, 2000, p.201). These last group believed that the passage of any resolutions and statements by international organization is more explanatory of governments function which are member of that organization rather than the organization itself, when electing about pros and cons of one resolution that poses some issues regarding international law, States are forming their own practice about the discussed issue or try to display own legal belief related to the matter. Therefore, it is better to know such a function more as a manifestation of State behavior and inclination than assessing

---

1. Advisory Opinion of Reservations to the Convention on the Prevention and Punishment of the Crime of Genocide, ICJ Reports, 1951, p.15.

organization practice (Ibid, p.202)

On this basis, act of United Nation in registration of nuclear fatwa can be indicative of UN practice in this matter, in addition, general secretary of UN in his bilateral session with Iran's supreme leader whereas showed his satisfaction in relation with issuance of nuclear fatwa, appreciated Iran's confidence-building measures. Also issuance of the resolution in supporting Iran and in condemnation of violence and extremism as double examples of WMD was another instance of UN in road of custom-making process of nuclear fatwa. In addition to UN, the other international organization and movements like; Islamic cooperation, African union, non-allied movement, International Atomic Energy Agency and world hygiene organization admired Iran for issuance of nuclear fatwa and directly or indirectly respected its nationally peaceful nuclear approach in several periods of time through several mechanisms; which symbolizes the custom-making practice of these organization[1].

Hence, international organizations as the main subjects of international law system can participate in practice-making process and forming of the rules of law, whether in the framework of inner organs and or in relation to other States at international relations level.

3.3.1.3. International Judicial Authorities:

International court and tribunals are not legislation authorities. The point that is needed to be noted here is that whether international judicial authorities themselves can make practice in the process of formation of international customary law or not? In other words, whether decisions of these authorities can be considered as "general practice" that constitutes the material element of custom? This issue can be represented from 3

---

1. For more information see the pictures.

perspectives. One is considering international court and tribunals as constitutions that take their competency and authorities from governments.

Thus, their verdicts are viewed as a form of State practice and another that consideration of this authorities as inner organs of an international organization and thus viewing their decisions as the approach of that organization and finally the judicial practice of judicial authorities that can find the presence of customary rules in different areas. In each 3 ways, the issue is that whether international courts and tribunals can be material element of custom-making practice?

Regarding this issue, some authors have considered these authorities decisions as a form of State delegation practice[1]. Professor Wolfke believes; this fact that States accept verdicts and ideas of judicial organs means that such decisions per se can be viewed as a form of State practice (Wolfke, 1993, p.74). In his viewpoint, such an idea also has been already affirmed by Guggenheim. Then Wolfke clearly has pointed out the international court of justice practice and accordingly analyses planned references of Court to its own prior decisions and also refers the other international constitutions including States themselves, international organizations, non-governmental organizations, international law commission and doctrine to such decisions in this framework (Ibid, p.74) From his view; it is completely natural that we assess judicial history in the framework of the international practice leading to formation of customary law. It has explicitly been accepted by States (Ibid, p.75). Wolfke even is in opposite of persons who believe in kind of made and polished law should be viewed (Ibid, p.75). Also, then some judgments of court are adduced by this lawyer to prove the claim. For example , Court in

---

1. Statement of Principles Applicable to The Formation of General Customary International Law, op. cit., Article 10, (Commentary).

the case of boundaries limitation of continental shelf between Canada/ US in 1984 has specified that (...Court verdict ...in the cases of North sea continental shelf has been considered as the greatest participation of this authority in application of governing customary law in the discussed area.)[1]

part D of paragraph 1 of Article 38 international Court of justice Statute that due to it(... judicial decisions ... as accessory tools to determine rules of law) is considered, also is another reason that has been posed by Wolfke regarding the practice-making role of international judicial authorities verdicts. He believes that this part of Article 38 indirectly guarantees the acceptance of some degrees of rulemaking by judicial authorities (Wolfke, 1993). Therefor in the context of custom making of nuclear fatwa, with referring to judiciary judgements of ICJ[2], we can refer to general practice of ICJ in acceptance of unilateral declarations in position of an international document, based on this fact and several verdicts of ICJ, nuclear fatwa as an unilateral declaration and based on customary practice of ICJ is recognised as an international evidence. Accordingly the unilateral measurements of other States in acceptance of nuclear fatwa is supported by international judiciary practice in road of custom-making process.

3.3.1.4. Non-governmental International Organizations:

Primarily does not accept governing doctrine, direct participation

---

1. Case concerning Delimitation of the Maritime Boundary in the Gulf of Maine Area, ICJ Reports, 1984, p.292

2. Nuclear Tests (Australia v. France; New Zealand v. France), I.C.J. Reports 1974, pp. 269-70, para. 51, and pp. 474-5, para. 53. Case concerning the Frontier Dispute (Burkina Faso v. Republic of Mali), I.C.J. Reports 1986, pp. 573-4, paras. 39-40. Case concerning Armed Activities on the Territory of the Congo (New Application: 2002) (Democratic Republic of the Congo v. Rwanda), Jurisdiction of the Court and Admissibility of the Application, para. 49.

of non-governmental international organizations in the making process of international customary law. Although the situation related to treaties is also the same. Non-governmental international organizations are not active subjects of international law and cannot cause right or obligation. They can merely be the subject of right of obligation. Unlike non-governmental international organizations that directly participate in the practice- making process leading to the formation of customary material element, role of non-governmental organizations is only limited to some secret lobbies in backstage and influence on State agents in diplomatic conferences and international assemblies[1]. Therefore, non-governmental organizations can play important roles in all steps related to the formation of customary law, from the beginning of the negotiations and reasons gathering to identifying and final ratification of rule, but they do not have direct participation in the process.

Also, - clearly about treaties- non-governmental organizations is possible to enter extensive strains on international society members to put a specific treaty draft in the agenda of future negotiations and or even, in some cases, it's possible to represent a specific draft text of own to be combined with the text that is developed by States(Hobe, 2005, p.213). But ultimately, it is these States – and not non-governmental organizations- that participate in the conclusion of treaties. The situation regarding customary international law norms that the above-mentioned organizations, with respect to them, can indirectly influence on governments function and their approach development (Ibid, p.214).

For example, International Red Cross (ICRC) that has had very efficient role in development and promotion of international

---

1. see: Fitzmaurice, M, *Actors and Factors in the Treaty-Making Process* ,Contemporary Issues in the Law of Treaties, pp.49,57-58, by Fitzmaurice, M, and Elias, eds, 2005.

humanitarian law. In some lawyers' viewpoint, any surveying of humanitarian law without any reference to International Red Cross will be deficient. Red Cross consisted of Red Cross International commission, Red Cross national societies, one coordinator center and Red Cross assembly. Red Cross International commission that each of the Geneva Conventions knows it as (a neutral International institution) is responsible for the development and exaltation of substantial humanitarian law. Nobody can ignore the role of this effective international constitution in the process of codification and ratification of the Geneva foursome Conventions in 1949, the ratified protocols of 1977 and other documents related to humanitarian law.

International law association that has been active from 1873 has had effective participation in the formation process of international rules. This organization participation in passage and making the rules related to armed conflicts– like Red Cross international organization – is one of its most important functions. International law association often presents some recommendations before formal codification of international rules. For example, it can be mentioned of 1963 resolutions about legal system governing on space beyond atmosphere leading to the conclusion of 1972 and 1967 treaties and or 1969 resolutions about campaign against sea pollution that after some months led to the conclusion of 1969 Conventions of Brussels in this area.

Viewing at the function of International law association, it can be stated that almost all the tasks of this organization lead to development of Conventions drafts and or issuance of resolutions that has been the basis for international rules formal codification (Ibid, p. 309). Nonetheless, it must emphasized again that International law association activity as a non- governmental constitution has been merely planning for possibility realization of generating international law rules and no direct participation is made in this framework. In this regard, the widespread support of NGOs from issuance of nuclear fatwa is very notable[1], because has this potential to be considered as a ground-maker tool in advent of a new legal regime in prohibition of threat, utilization and proliferation of WMD.

3.3.2. Nature of Practice:

3.3.2.1. Verbal and Material Acts:

Generally counting practices and behavior that guarantee international practice leading to the formation of customary rule is not a simple task. Primarily, material elements or practice can include both physical and material act of States and verbal act of them. Nevertheless, lawyers' view regarding this issue is not the same because some of the related specialists accept only physical acts as practice, while it seems that dominant view about this issue regarding international judicial practice indicate any kind of behavior as the material element custom-formation .Then, we will continue this discussion in detail.

As it mentioned, there is a disagreement concerning the nature of State practice – like other posed issues in the present writing. Some lawyers like Damato and Wolfke view only State material and physical acts as a manifestation of the practice and representing a strict concept regarding this issue, limit the source range of custom's material element. They believe that any claims or general statements per se cannot be explanatory of State practice. In this regard professor Damato asserts; a claim is not an act. Although the claims may articulate a legal norm, they can't constitute the material component of custom. (Damato, 1971, p88)

According to him, sending missiles, nuclear procedures, receiving ambassadors, making levies on customs duties, expelling

---

1. For more information see the pictures and indexes.

an alien, capturing a pirate vessel, setting up a drilling rig in the continental shelf, visiting and searching a neutral ship and …are among the most important State's practices. For a State has not done anything when it makes a claim; until it takes enforcement action, the claim has little value as a prediction of what the State will actually do(idem). The situation is the same in the cases that a State decides to support or oppose the development or changing of an act. Damato provides an example in this regard; sending the first Sputning to the globe and at the same time the development of the customary law related to passing the satellite over other countries' territories.

He believes that if a State's decision was to oppose the development of this law, it was necessary for the States to show this either by providing a constraint for passing the aforementioned satellite, or in the case of lack of ability to do this by any way to act against the Soviet Union (idem, p89). Also Damato pays attention to the possibility of difference between the actions and words of States. If our understanding of practice component implies both physical and verbal behavior, we might occasionally face with the issue that there is a difference between what the State says and acts.Basically, this difference will not exist if we consider practices as physical acts. The State can say many things with different voices at the one time but a State can act in only one way at one time (idem, p 51). In addition to Damato, Professor Wei provides nearly the same analysis about the practice component. In his opinion, providing a great commentary of what would be the material component of custom including the placing of different verbal acts such as unilateral intimations, declarations, statements, resolutions, and treaties and… in this framework, only leads to the increase of ambiguities.

Specially, in regard of Wolfke's view point and other similar views; there is no reason for not paying attention to the verbal acts or general declarations of the States. In this regard, hinting to the professor Mullerson's ideas would be logical. Although he will not show clearly the component of the actions that comprise the States practice, he puts the acceptance of the wide concept of the evidences that formulate material component of the custom against the same challenge, as was put by Damato.

At first he acknowledges that there is a distinction between what the States claim and what the States act. For example, the "the claim" of having the right of innocent passage in waters of a territory and it's "enforcement". But he asserts that in the case of acceptance of the wide definition of practice, what would be the way to distinguish it from the legal beliefs of the States? (Mullerson, 1998, p 161) In this regard also Red considers the distinction between act and legal belief where verbal acts are paid attention as the reason for creating practices. Nevertheless, Mullerson does not clearly assert that he agrees with the acceptance of verbal acts as the State's practices or not. Finally, he States his analysis this way, that the State's practice can contain both subjective component [verbal acts] and the objective component [physical acts] but the subjective component is not always defined as legal belief (idem). Mullerson believes that subjective attitudes of the States about their act may be implied in their actions (idem). Specifically, about the attitudes of Professor Thirlway, the acts of the States, foundations and international judicial authorities, show that simply general statements and declarations without considering any special situation, can be paid attention as evidences for creating the material component of custom and as previously mentioned, basically, the framework that this lawyer poses for the acceptance of verbal acts of the States, is not logical and real. Also professor Mendelson is among the other lawyers that states effectively about the contribution of the verbal acts in the process of the formation of international customary law.

By providing lists of the actions that are often cited as the evidences for making practices, he explicitly emphasizes that there is no greater reason which shows why the general statements of the States besides their physical actions should not be regarded as a form of State practices (Mendelson, 1998, p205).

Totally, diplomatic statements including complaints and declarations which show the State policy, State counsel advice , press releases, statute books and official instructions related to juridical issues such as the instructions related to the military law, participation in voting in the international organizations, State remarks about the projects which are under the consideration of the international law commission and other similar institutions, national legislation, decision of domestic courts, bills before the international Courts and so on are examples of the States' actions which Mandelson believes that they contribute to the process of practice-making which lead to the formation of the material component of custom(idem,p204). Under the influence of the professor Mendelson's viewpoints, International law association's statement about the principles governing the formation of customary law, has considered the verbal acts as the State's practice. Article 4 of the declaration States:"verbal acts of the States, not only the physical acts, are also considered as the State's practice." according to the association, in the interpretation of this article, verbal acts mean statements or general declarations which in fact form a commoner shape of the State's practice in comparison to the physical act.

Diplomatic statements(such as complaints), political statements, press releases, official instructions(such as military law) , armed forces' circular, States' interpretations about the drafts of the treaties , domestic legislation, votes of the national courts and executive authorities, the views of the governments before international courts, international organizations' statements and resolutions and so on are all examples of the verbal acts.

Thus, international law association besides Akehurst and Mendelson discusses the quality of participation of verbal acts similar to the physical acts in the process of practice-making which lead to the formation of the material component of custom. Finally it acknowledges despite of the content above, we can consider some of the declarations more usefully as just stating the beliefs than the official acts of the State's practice. Professor Dinstein believes a view which only considers physical acts as the component of custom, is a highly exaggerated view (Dinstein, 2003, p215).

This jurist believes this is right that in a wide level a physical act is of a greater importance in comparison to a verbal announcement, warning, or censures (totally verbal acts) however, there is no difference between them in terms of their validity. Actually Dinstein considers a higher value for some actions such as laws authorized by parliaments and the votes issued by the courts than other verbal acts. In his opinion, undoubtedly, laws authorized by legislative institutions and domestic courts' decisions have a higher value like physical acts —or even more value — in the process of practice-making, however, in other cases the general declarations of the States including statements, announcements and notices, only have a side role (idem) and they cannot make an practice which leads to the formation of the material component of custom without the States' physical acts (idem, p 276).

Thus although at first, he considers physical and verbal acts of the States in the same way, finally, he makes some distinctions between them in relation to their role quality in the process of practice-making which lead to the creation of customary rules. Yet this dissociation is not at all comparable to the Twirl Wee viewpoints who considered totally verbal acts as the evidences for making practices. Dinstein believes in this framework, when the preconditions are available, the general statements of the States can put their actions in a special situation, especially by making clarification of that action or by making explanation of that as an exception to the rule. In other words, there would be a kind of impact on the delimitation of the discussed rule. But this cannot contribute to the process of making the quantitative component of custom on its own (idem, p 277). Besides the judicial practices, international law association in the year 1950 clearly mentions treaties, domestic courts' decisions, national rules, diplomatic correspondences and national legal advisors' beliefs as examples of the possible different forms of the State practice, as well[1]. Also the States' considerations especially great States imply the acceptance of verbal acts as a kind of the State practice.

Declarations of the rights of foreign relations of the United States (section 102) states; actions and diplomatic instructions and other governmental acts and official statements whether they have been taken unilaterally or in a form of collaboration with other States ,for example in the framework of international organizations, they can establish different forms of the States' practice[2]. Relying on the verbal acts of the States in order to search for the customary law is the current reality of the international system and is of great importance, especially, for those States which do not have the material facilities for taking actions in a special field.

For example, for the States which do not have the weapons for mass destruction or the States which do not have the facilities for sending satellites to the space or landlocked States, verbal act is the only way of practice for them. As highlighted above, The International Court of Justice has consistently cited official

---
1. Yearbook of International Law Commission, 1950, pp.368-372.
2. The American Law Institute: *Restatement (Third) Foreign Relations Law of The United States, op-cit.,* para. 102, Comment b.

correspondences, diplomatic declarations and other similar cases and the States have not objected to them.

As it mentioned, practice can enjoy both material and oral aspects, in both hypothesis, custom-making process towards consolidation of legal regime of nuclear fatwa is attainable; because first, official representatives of several States mostly in high levels and in different diplomatic and non-diplomatic events supported[1] issuance of nuclear fatwa and its derived disarmament system repeatedly and by this way manifested the approach of their State about this legal regime. In practice, also with several measures like assistance in completion of Iran's nuclear establishment played a major role. Based on our triple assumptions from mechanisms of custom-making process of fatwa, these practices play a determinative role in this process.

3.3.2.2. Verbal Element; Emergence in the Practice or Legal Belief?

As was stated, the majority attitude toward the defining the nature of material component of custom contains both physical and verbal acts. Here the problem is that when verbal acts are considered as both the practice evidences and legal belief evidences, what would be the way to authenticate and dissociate them? Verbal acts are being considered as the most important evidence for proving the existence of legal belief. The result which is achieved in this case, according to some lawyers, will be an epistemological way which causes one of the components of the creator of the customary International law rule look redundant. Viewing more meticulously, the solving of problem does not seems to be difficult.

Although apparently and at first, considering verbal acts as evidences for both creating practice and evidences for creating

---

1. For more information see the pictures.

legal belief of the States, can lead to the fomenting of some ambiguities, these problems can appear where the States do not have any verbal act about an issue. In the recent case- besides the material component-also the mental component is extracted on the basis of the wide and convincing practice of the States and not through understanding of the preconceived notions. This has been expressly confirmed in the votes of the Court Branch in the year 1984 (Gulf of Maine case).[1] Thus necessarily, insisting on the dissociation between the sources of the evidences of components of custom is not logical. As the verbal acts can show the States practices and also the legal beliefs, physical acts can also contain such situations but in the case of the former we face a different situation.

In this regard some of the lawyers, in addition to acknowledging that verbal acts of the States can be cited as a form of practice, they believe that the contents of such actions will also show the mental elements or their legal beliefs. (Mendelson, 2000, p 206). In their opinion, our classification of a special verbal act as an example of a mental element or a material element depends on the situation (idem). But actually in some situations it is not possible to consider a special verbal act as a material element or legal belief of the States, because it might happen that in an issue –like force- we face with a massive amounts of verbal actions. Thus in such cases, it is necessary to consider the dual elements at the heart of the action and in mixing with each other. In the way that just considering taking actions in order to issue the verbal act such as issuing a statement or issuing a diplomatic announcement, participation in voting to issue resolution in the framework of the international organizations, participation in negotiations related to drafting a treaty or International Conventions and taking actions

---

1. *Case* concerning Delimitation of the Maritime Boundary in the Gulf of Maine Area, op.Para.111.

in order to ratify it and ... as the material element and the content of the mentioned instruments also show the mental element of legal belief of the States.

In status above that in some cases distinguish between words as a practice with words as a legal belief is difficult, in hypothesis of custom-making process of nuclear fatwa by verbal confirmation of international authorities, verbal statements are both practice-maker and indicative of their legal belief. (Seivanizad, 2013)

3.3.2.3. Refusal or Omission:

Although the material element or practice implies the States' actions(both physical and verbal), it is possible that under especial situations, refusing to take action(refusal) will be paid attention as a kind of the State's practice in the process of the formation of legal international customary rules. For example, refusal to prosecute an accused or suspect foreigner diplomat for committing the crime in order to create the customary rules related to the diplomatic immunities. The majority of the authors and commentators have more or less accepted the role of refusal in the process of making practices, professor Wolfke believes that "There is no basis for excluding refusal as a kind of process which lead to the formation of the international custom. Everything depends on the situation and occasion." (Wolfke, 1993. P61) Professor Akehurst also states "The State's practice can contain refusal and silence."(Akehurst, 1994, p11) The viewpoints of other jurists such as Sorensen, Tunkin, Bernhardt, Danilenko and Kunz, in relation to the role of refusal are the same.

In this way professor Mendelson also believes that; refusal can be paid attention as the material component of custom or practice but we should consider the situation and a degree of caution (Mendelson, 2000.p207). Like other jurists such as Wolfke and Akehurst, he poses popular Lutos vote as the basis of his analysis.

168 It appears that the best understanding of the role and place of the refusal in the process of making practices which lead to the formation of customary rules, have been done in the framework of this idea. In this case, The Permanent Court of International Justice did not accept the refusal of the States (except the flag State) from the prosecuting of the accidents on high seas as an evidence for existing a customary legal international rule which ban the States from such actions(idem).

But this policy of The Court was for the reason that the refusals of the States were ambiguous and this can mean that there is no problem in situations that refusals of the States as a government practice contain no ambiguity. In this case, by citing to the lack of prosecution from the non-flag States about the claims related to the collision on the high seas, The French government was a pretender of a kind of duty for such States. The Permanent Court of Justice denies this reasoning of the French government not because of the fact that refusals of the States naturally do not have the characteristic to consider this as an "practice", but because this refusal seemed ambiguous in such situation and it was unlikely that this was as a result of aware commitment. Mendelson believes that in this case, there could be other reasons for refusal which basically have nothing to do with the International law. For example, the lack of authority or jurisdiction by virtue of domestic law (most of the criminal rules are constrained in the territory), or lack of interest and believe in the fact that the flag State is in a better situation for prosecution and punishment of the crime.

In this framework, there is another similar practice in the vote of the International Court of Justice about the legality of the threat or using of nuclear weapons in 1996 when the Court denies this reasoning: Since the states that have nuclear weapons, have prevented from using them from 1945, so they have accepted the commitment of not using them[1].

Although here the Court denies the possibility of the emergence of a rule on the basis of the States' refusal, this does not mean that the court disagrees with the acceptance of refusal as a way of the State's practice and the reason is that the political situation (prevention) is responsible for not using the weapons in the mentioned period (idem). In other words, if the situation does not contain any ambiguity, considering refusal as a kind of the State's practice would be possible; if the refusal of the States which have nuclear weapons from using this kind of weapons showed clearly the legal votes of the States, the Court could well extract a customary rule about this issue. In connection with recent expression, that is an important point to be considered that, as non-realization of an act can include an omission, non-realization of a verbal act also can include a legal refusal. Therefore, with regard to non-hearing of any condemnation against nuclear fatwa and its derived legal regime by internationally official authorities, it can be found out the existence of custom-making process even with refusal mechanism by non-active States. (Seivanizad, 2013)

3.3.3. Characteristics of the Practice:

Which characteristics should the practice or material component of custom have? Under which quality are the States' actions recognized as the international practice? Article 38 (1) (b) of the Statute of the International Court of Justice only considers the generality of the practice. Nevertheless, investigating of the jurists ideas about the international juridical practice implies other traits and qualities which the practice that lead to the formation of a customary rule should also contain them. We will discuss this issue in detail in this section.

---

1. Case concerning Legality of the Threat or Use of Nuclear Weapons, op. cit., para. 67.

3.3.3.1. The Generality of Practice and the Limits of This Generality:

As previously mentioned especially in citing the paragraph1 (b) of the article 38 of the Statute of the International Court of Justice, the international practice which lead to the formation of the customary law should be "general". But this generality does not mean the participation of all States in the world in the process of the practice-making, because in this way we should wait for years for creating a customary law to come true that is so exceptional and far away from expectation. With the generality of the practice, it means that it implies "wideness" and "similarity" which are the basis for the formation of the rule and all of the States are required to comply with them, unless it be in the framework of " Persistent Objector[1] ". The general practices of the States contain both the sequential and parallel actions which are as a result of the practices of cognizable organizations in a period. In most of the cases these actions can be accomplished independently, however, the consistency between the States should not be disregarded. Now we should discuss about the issue that how many States should participate in this practice?

There is no specific criterion in this regard and naturally like the other issues about the custom, it is difficult to exactly pose a rule about the number of the States which should participate in the practice which leads to the formation of the customary law. This participation not only contains the States actions but also it contains the reactions of other States whose interests are affected. (Akehurst, 1974, p16). The majority of the customary rules which have been done by the international juridical authorities were based on the wide participation of the States.

---

1. See: Dinestein, Yoram, op, cit., p.285
Also: Statement of Principles Applicable to The Formation of General Customary International Law, op. cit., Article 15(a)

But it is also possible that the general practices of the States be the result of the actions of a few numbers of the countries. And it is also possible that the other States have the "once in each direction" participation. (Dinestein, 2006, p283) But it has been said that if a State or a group of States do not protest against the action of another group in the case that they are objector to that, their silence mean that they have accepted such actions. (Idem) From the standpoint of international Law association committee statement about the principles governing the formation of the international customary law , the States practices should be wide in order to create a general rule of the international customary law, so as was stated in the court's practice, and not necessarily universal[1], also it is not necessary for the specific governmental requirements to an international customary law, it will be proven that the mentioned State has participated in the practice actively or deliberately has agreed about that (idem). And the international judicial authorities has never denied this State from the commitment for the reason that the State has not participated actively in the practice which lead to the formation of General rule of customary international law claims.(idem).

As it was considered, the alliance of all States in custom-making process of something is not necessary, rather only by positive alliance of some States and even by their silence possibility of custom-making process is possible, so the widespread support of several States from the legal regime of nuclear fatwa has provided enough quantity in order to form a related international customary rule.

3.3.3.2. The Time Element:

Custom is formed within time (Dinestein, 2006, p293).

---

1. Statement of Principles Applicable to The Formation of General Customary International Law, op. cit., *Article 14(1)*.

How much time is necessary for a customary law to come into emergence? About this we should state that there is no specific criterion. Maybe in this frame work; the time needed for the time passing for creating a customary law; the wording of the International Court of Justice in North Sea Continental Shelf Cases will be the best criterion for analyzer.

Although passing a short time does not necessarily or in itself prevent the formation of the customary rule of international law, on the basis of what was basically a convention rule, but the necessary condition in this short period is that the practices of the States especially those States whose interest will have been affected especially, regarding the citation of the regulation, be wide and really consistent. In addition to this, the practice should be made so that it makes possible the recognition of the fact that a legal rule or a legal necessity has been regarded[1]. The needed scale of time continuity in order to creation of an international customary rule depends on various related factors. For example, if an issue was stated which no other rule was accepted about that, establishing the rules concerning the issue will take shorter time than the issue which exist a customary law for it and it should be adjusted for the establishment of the new rule. Nowadays, in parallel of the development of the international relations, the importance of time is reduced .In assessing the behavior of a State, time is of low importance and its situation in each case depends on the other factors related to that activity. In the past and in the Roman law, basically custom was considered as a product of a long practice, also in the common law in order to convert the practice to law, that practice should have a long history insofar as nobody can remember its root time. (Mendelson, 2000, p209). In the international level, most of the legal rules have a long history .but this does not mean that the formation of the new rules also

---

1. Case concerning North Sea Continental Shelf, op. cit., *p. 43*.

need such history.

At present, the creations of the customary rules are provided in a short time and faster than the past (idem, p210). For example the rules governing the law of sea were first announced by President Truman in the year 1945.[1] In the year of 1951, in the judgement of the Abu Dhabi Lord Asquitli the dispute case of Petroleum Company of Dolapment and Sheikh Abu Dhabi, he ruled that the mentioned doctrine with specific line yet do not appear in the international stature of a rule of law[2]. But over the next years and until the 958 Geneva Conference , more States claimed jurisdiction over the continental shelf.at the time of the conference had been accepted that the coastal States should have especial rules over their continental shelf. And thus 1958 convention recognized such rights for the coastal States. Therefore, in connection with nuclear fatwa - that in form has structural-legal affinity with Truman declaration- with regard to passage of more than a decade from its issuance, seems that the process of its custom-making has entered the new phase.

3.3.3.3. Integrity and Uniformity of Practices:

The practice should be Virtually Uniform in order to participate

---

1. In this year, the president of the united states, announced the jurisdiction and control over the continental shelf.".... *The government of the United States considers the natural resources of the continental shelf waters as then possessions of the Unites States and under its jurisdiction and control."*
What was mentioned here was a clear statement of the idea of belonging the continental shelf to the coastal state? A unilateral claim which gained support later from the other States which have important interest in the area of the continental shelf and finally it converted into a customary rule of international law. The completion of this process lasted for several years.
2. Petroleum Development (Trucial Const) Ltd. v. Sheikh of Aim Dhabi, *International Law* Reports, 1951, p. 155.

in the process of making the principles of international law[1]. It means that the different samples of the practice, should necessarily be similar and consistent both internally and in general[2]. That the practice should be internally consistent means that the behavior of a participated State in the process of custom-making about a special issue should be consistent in different levels. By consistency in general, it means that different States should not have different practices about a special issue (idem). In the Nicaragua case, the court did not find an opportunity to consider come points in relation to the present issue. According to The Court when considering customary international law related to the principle of banning on the resort to the force and also the principle of prevention from intervening of the States in each other's internal affairs, this international juridical institution do not expect that the States' practice in obeying the mentioned principles to be in a high rate so that they should prevent from intervention in each other's affairs by resorting to force in a consistent way.

The Court believes that for the formation of a customary law, it is not necessary that the related practice be consistent with that rule. In order to establish the existence of such a rule, it will be enough that the States' behaviors be generally consistent with that and the examples of the practice which are inconsistent and incompatible with the rule, should be treated as a violation of that rule and not the signs indicating the recognition of a new rule[3]. As was considered, no certainty has been prescribed based on the complete implementation of a same practice by international law, so that the practice of States in order to consolidate legal regime of nuclear fatwa, mostly in verbal form, include from direct hint

---
1. *Case* concerning North Sea Continental Shelf, op. cit., *p.43*.
2. Statement of Principles Applicable to The Formation of General Customary International Law, op. at., *Article 13*.
3. Case concerning Military and Paramilitary Activities in and against Nicaragua, op. cit., *para.183*-186.

on fatwa to confirmation of Iran's peaceful nuclear policies.

3.3.3.4. The Practice of the Beneficiary States:

The wide and consistent practice of the States in order to form a customary law, should be represented. International Court of Justice in the issues related to the continental shelf of The North Sea has emphasized on the" the practices of the States whose benefits are affected in a special way" in the process of practice-making.[1]

This suggests that the number of the States in comparison to the situation and the States which are related to the issue is of lower importance because their benefits are in relation to the mentioned rule. For a claim rule to legitimate, a proper reaction from the states and the beneficiary States is needed. Thus for example we can hint to the Britain's contribution in the formation of the law of the sea in the nineteenth century and the role of the United States and the former Soviet Union in the development of the law beyond the atmosphere. Before a claim rule can find its way in the area of the customary international law, it is possible that the participation of some States to be more necessary. What is meant by this; is the realization of an affirmative practice of the nuclear States in custom-making process of the legal regime of nuclear fatwa, i.e. non (nuclear, chemical & microbial) States basically play no role in utilization or non-utilization of WMD to want to be effective in respect to such custom, however, they can take an effective step by their affirmative acts. In this respect, remarkable welcome of powerful nuclear States[2] like: China, Russia, USA, India and Pakistan from issuance of nuclear fatwa has accelerated the formation process of a new custom derived from the legal regime of fatwa.

---

1. Case concerning North Sea Continental Shelf, op. cit., *para.74*.
2. For more information see the pictures.

3.4. Opinio Juris

As previously mentioned and in the definition; one of the component elements of custom is the immaterial element which reflects the legal belief of the States in following of a practice. Now the discovery of this legal belief can be obtained through different ways which are discussed here[1].

3.4.1. Concept and Necessity

3.4.1.1. Concept

As the International Court of Justice states in the issues related to the continental shelf of the North Sea, in the formation of the customary rules, merely the existence of a "great" and "much unified" practice is not enough. Also the mentioned practice should be made in a way that it implies the recognition of legal rules or obligations. In this regard the Court explains that "two conditions should be met": first the existence of "an established practice" which contain the mentioned conditions and the other" belief in the fact that such practice is obligatory because of the existence of a legal law"[2]. Thus, the objective element of custom-practice- as was mentioned in the previous part, should accompany with a" Subjective Element" which lies in the concept

---

1. Opinio Juris issue is seriously debatable in the customary law. according to some of the analyzers, the exact defining of the psychological element in the process of making custom, possibly has created more academic debates and discussions in comparison to the whole claims based on the custom rules. (Thirlway, H, International Customary Law and Codification, op. cit., p.47) this statement actually mean that the current issue in the world, rather than providing a challenge in the legal relations, provides the grounds for a wide debate in academic areas. (Statement of Principles Applicable to The Formation of General Customary International Law, op. cit., Part III (comment 2)).
2. Cose concerning North Sea Continental Shelf, op. cit., p.44.

of the "legal beliefs derived from necessities[1]" .the Latin equivalent which is usually used as an abbreviation:"Opinio Juris", "the legal beliefs of the States" or in others view point "legal firm vote of the States" (Falsafi, 1386, p539). Such a concept dissociates the Wheat from the practice or Chaff. (Dinestein, 2006.p293) Thus the aforementioned practice should be drawn in the form of the following equation.

The general practice of the States + their legal belief = custom = International law; so the existence of both objective and subjective elements of custom- meaning the general practice and legal belief- is necessary and unavoidable in the process of making the legal rules. The first element defines what has occurred in the world and the second element prescribes the entering of the existing practice to the legal relations era (right and duty) (Estern, 2001, p91). Also it should be noted that in a way that practice which lead to the formation of the customary rule should be general, the legal belief needed in this process should also have the necessary generality. In other words, the legal belief should also be the product of belief or shared attitude of the States of the world or the international community as a whole. And this is different from the individual legal belief of the States.

Accordingly what is certain is that the legal belief of States to the inhumanity of consequences resulting from utilization of WMD, is an universal belief, hence the formation of a custom based on the legal regime of nuclear fatwa- that has prescribed the certain inhibition of WMD- from this view, is completely obvious and undeniable.

3.4.1.2. Necessity

Basically the States behavior lie in their relation to each other in different forms. Some of the behaviors may accompany a legal

---

1. Opinio Juris sive necessitates

necessity and some others do not. If it is supposed that some behaviors become the custom, the condition is that what is legally necessary (what is necessary in accompany with the legal belief) should be divided from what is not necessary. Also there are some cases in which the behavior or in other words the practice which should be considered in the process of making the customary rules, is ambiguous. (Idem)[1] Also in these cases the legal beliefs of the Sates have gained attention as a decisive concept especially from the international Court of Justice in order to explain the issue that why the practices of the mentioned States were not regarded in the process of making custom. A behavior that does not clearly have the ability to refer to an existing or potential legal treaty or in other words does not fit in the framework of international legal relations, should not be paid attention in making or defining a f a existence of a general customary rule, One of these cases in the ambiguous refusals. As was mentioned in the previous sections, the actions which are based on the refusal have the capability that in a state of the necessary conditions, participate like the positive actions in the process of making rules. One of these conditions is the necessary clearance for recognition of the action. One of these conditions is crystallization for the recognition of the act. But even if this comes true, theoretically and practically in most of the cases the refusals are ambiguous. And what can make clear these ambiguities are the legal beliefs of the States.

3.4.2. Nature

Especially the content of the discussion here is based on the question that in the process of formation of custom, on which basis and why should the States continue doing that? By States. I mean the States which act in a systematic way and in a specific framework. In this regard, interpreters and the followers of

---

1. (par IV)

different schools of thought, offer different explanations which can be divided into two groups: 1) The theory of the implied consent of the voluntarist, 2) Legal belief derived from the necessities.

3.4.2.1. The Consent Theory of the Voluntarist

It has been considered by them from the Grotius time that what explicitly is in consent of the States is treaty and what is done implicitly is customary law. And this is rooted in Positivism. The advocates of the voluntarist theory of custom generally put their establishment on the basis that; since the States have government in the international relations area, they are not required to the obligations without their consent. In their idea, custom is regarded as a kind of implied treaty which the States have to follow if they have created that. Tunkin –one of the advocates of this theory- believes that "the basis of the customary rules, is the consistency of voluntarism of the countries or other subjects of the international law. The countries have the same right in the process of making international law rules and so the majority of them cannot make the rules which is necessary for the small numbers of countries to follow." (Arechaga,1978.p10)

He considers accepting a view point other than this, contradictory with the principal rules of international law. In law- although not in the world- the States have the same value. It is right that in reality this tendency of the powerful States to determine the actual influence on the process of the formation of international law, legally, the majority of the States cannot create rules for the others and consider them obligatory for them to follow. Tonkin continues this is of great importance that the situation is different especially in the current international law system whose duty is to adjust the relations between the States belonging to different social system. Only a rule has the capability to convert into general international law rule which has been recognized in all of the legal systems by the States (Walden, 1977). But this theory has a wide range of objections. In this regard Kelsen believes that "the customary law is necessary to obey for the countries who have not participated in the customary law and the idea that this is just necessary to obey for the countries who have recognized the laws, is on the basis of an international norm.[1] " In fact, if this theory will become in to practice in a flexible and permanent way, its practical consequences will be out of mind.

Among the implied consent theorists, professor Strupp maintains interesting view. At first he believes that "agreement" in the only possible source in the international law, Provided that the States are equal to each other, and if there is not a great organization and no top authority to impose a rule on the States, accordingly we can conclude that the international law cannot exist without consent and consistent voluntarists of the States (Straff, 1934, p301). Strupp considers custom as implied consent that implied satisfaction and this is the interesting point of his view, and a State is necessary to obey the other States who have admitted the claim rule. It seems this theory based on manner of presentation of a suggestion to apply a regulation, has somewhat theoretic affinity in road of consolidation of the legal regime derived from nuclear fatwa, because the agreed States with this regime that indicates their implied satisfaction, make them committed to non(utilization, proliferation and stockpiling) of WMD.

3.4.2.2. Legal Beliefs Derived From the Necessities

Literally this expression means a belief or legal belief derived from the necessities; The Latin equivalent of this show that it has no roots in the Roman law and in the classical writings (idem,

---

1. Kelsen, Hans, Principles of International Law, Johns Hopkins University, 1967, pp.44-45.

p262). It appears that the first person who has used this expression completely, is the 1389 Genny contract.(D'amato,1971.p49) and this is in the domestic law framework although in Guggenheim idea, some parts of this idea or other ideas similar to that are found in the written history of Germany in the late eighteenth century (Mendelson, 2000, p286). In the current discussion, generally the expression Opinio Juris Sive neessitates is interpreted as "belief in the legal nature and necessary related act (practice), or belief in its necessity. " In other words, a State which makes a practice or procedure, believes that it does a kind of legal obligatory or it accepts a legal right that this obligation and right is also" is the manifestation of an objective rule and is based on the social life requirements and international life necessities". (Hekmat,1347,p138).

Accordingly Kelsen believes that the customary law is necessary for the States which have not participated in the creation of customary rule-including new and also the active States- and this idea that the international law is just necessary for the countries who have recognized its law-as was stated by the voluntarists view- is on the basis of a norm of international law. Based on this school, the hypothesis of formation of custom emanating from legal regime of nuclear fatwa is not unavailable, because based on this school, existence of a necessity related to international life necessities, is a fundamental term in determination of States legal belief in adherence to obeying a practice, with such an explanation, is there any necessity in dreams of international law to be more important than maintenance of international peace and security ?consequently, recognizing the element of necessity in explaining the nature of custom-making process of legal regime of fatwa is decisive.

3.4.3. Status of the Principles and Fundamental Rules

It is needed to explain that in the international system, some of the rules have a position that the international community do not have doubt in considering them as a part of general international law corpus and so juridical institutes did not conduct a research from the view point of the recognition of the material and immaterial elements of it.

For example the International Court of Justice with using the expressions such as "important principles of the international law", "the fundamental principles of international law", " a part of modern international law", " the approved and recognized rules of the international law", and son on, has considered these rules certain and has not accepted a special trend for proving the. The Permanent International Court of Justice also had the same situation. That the Court has taken action to the recognition of the rule according to the procedure that it has defined in its judicial practice and we will investigate that as a part of international law, does not mean that the court was ignorant about the recognition of the component element of custom, but these rules have been refrained from more research because of the popularity and the certainty of these rules. In other words"certain practice" and "certain belief" are the existing conditions of a customary rule that the court imagines them in relation to some rules from the view point of the mentioned characteristics, and then starts to recognize the rule. Also the principles such as the supremacy of international law on domestic law[1] and the obligatory of unilateral action[2], which undoubtedly are among the accepted principles and certain principles of general international law in the judicial international practice, have been recognized.

On this basis and with regard to advent of some fundamental

PCIJ, Series A, 1928, No.9, & PCIJ, Series A, 1926, No.7 P.31.1
2. Nuclear Tests Case, ICJ Reports, 1974, (New Zeland/France), para45, and (Australia/France), para.42.

rules such as inhibition of genocide, crime against humanity and war crimes which has been embodied in the legal regime of nuclear fatwa, recognizing the Opinio Juris in practice of agreed States is not necessary.

3.5. The Recognition of a Customary Law with Relying on the Central Role of Legal Belief

As mentioned, the principal approach of the judicial practice in the process of recognition of customary international law was based upon considering the practice and then recognize and discover its legal belief. In other words, the judicial practice has searched for the legal beliefs of the States by relying on the States' practices. But it is necessary to mention that taking such procedures could not be effective in all cases. The developments of the international communities under the influence of development of the humanistic concepts and human rights suggest that in the process of recognition of related necessary legal rules, another procedure should be taken. In such area, the mentioned process can never be based on because in most of the cases, at first, or there is no practice or what is available is contradictory and inconsistent. Therefore and on this basis The International Court of Justice takes another trend in order to recognize the customary rules related to the humanistic considerations especially the humanitarian law, takes another trend into consideration which is usually referred to as practice or modern attitude in the procedure of recognition of customary rules. We will discuss about this issue later.

3.5.1. Recognition of the Concept and Review of Some Theoretical Concepts:

3.5.1.1. Concept and Origin:

Although the process of the concept and the origin of its formation and recognition of the rule is a pre-determined process and is based upon a two-element system, is never done in a consistent and exact way. The judicial international practice shows that the judicial institutions have followed the mentioned practice when recognizing the rule without considering the pre-defined general system and because of taking into consideration the situation and also the judicial policy which is affected by variables such as shared regulation, justice and benefit and is different from situation to situation. And it is certainly due to the positive and great attribute of custom as a source of fluid with the high adjustability capability which can continuously adjust itself to the transition of the international community. It appears that the source of such adjustment in judicial practice should be searched through the reaction of The International Court of Justice in recognition of Article 3 common to the four Geneva Conventions in the case of Nicaragua.

Way of identifying the shared 3 article in the court's vote show that this judicial institution has excluded consideration of the States' practices at first and has considered a central and dominant role for the legal beliefs of the States in the recognition process and this procedure of the court became a pattern for other international judicial institutions which recognized in this way their customary rules in their own competence. We should also mention that in the new procedure framework, the legal beliefs of the States are derived from Principles of Humanity and Dictates of the public Conscience and not from their practice. In other words, a belief which is not in the framework of the States voluntary and their national benefits but is influenced by most of the principles and natural valuable laws and ideas. In this field, the recognition of the legal belief (in relation to the necessity of a rule) is imagines upon those Principles of Humanity and Dictates of the public Conscience which undoubtedly are acceptable by all members of the international community and then its following is investigated in the State's practice. In this framework "The Court should convince that the existence of the rule in the legal beliefs of the States, is emphasized in their practice.[1] " The contradiction and conflict in the State's practice can undermine the laws based upon the practice, however, in the case of the laws dependent upon the humanistic and moral values-here modern customary law- the situation is different and the contradictory practices do not question its validity (Roberts, 2001, p765). And this can be a positive attribute for the new procedure in which the natures of the formed and recognized rules have the eternal stability and consistency.

Also sometimes the modern procedure has been compared with the interpretation of Hardt and Koskenniemi[2]. The prescriptive interpretation of Hardt about law and the Utopian interpretation of Koskenniemi about law, on the basis of the first interpretation, laws are not resulted from considering the events and their descriptive because these facts imply what exists (the current practice). But in the light of this interpretation, the legal rules are always prescriptive and are wholly based upon what they should be (the practice which should exist)[3]. In the form of the second interpretation also law is based upon the principles which are not related to the States' benefits or their will; completely moral principles and different from their current reality which is imposed on the world. The general common joint of the criticisms on modern procedure implies on the ignoring of the dominant role and great role of the States' practices which causes

---

1. Case concerning Military and Paramilitary Activities in and against Nicaragua, op., cit., para.184.
2. *Ibid,* pp.761, 766.
3. Hart. H. L, A, The Concept of Law, Oxford University Press, 1961, p. 183.

the elimination of the international law by its destabilization albeit it's consistency with justice (Hoffmann, 2006, p20). But this is not the whole story.

The modern custom albeit all the criticisms about that, actually contains firm bases and because of that it has been accepted in the procedure of legal rulemaking as a new procedure. The acceptance of such a procedure is in fact a reaction to the issue that the existing traditional system could not meet the requirements of the international community in all cases. But where is its root and base? In other words, on what basis is the acceptance of a new attitude in the process of recognition of the customary rules of international law? As previously mentioned, in the new attitude, the recognition of the rule is based upon the initial and central proof of the legal beliefs of the States, a belief which is not derived from the practice but is derived from the humanity principles (principles derived from the authority beyond the States' will).

In this regard, the writer believes that although the transitions in the attitude of the court is affected by transitions related to the development of humanitarian concepts, but it origin should be because of the drafting and approval of the Martens clause in international community. That was an announcement in which the world accepted that in the field of humanistic considerations, the formation of the rule can be done under the influence of the dominant principles and natural law ideas. It was an announcement whose ratification and issue was under the influence of the transitions resulted from the development of the principles and bases of human rights especially in the early nineteenth century and the article 3 common to the four Geneva conventions that was mentioned before is somehow the manifestation of this clause which the court has considered humanistic considerations at first and it means the direct affecting of the law basis in the process of formation and transition of custom.

3.5.1.2. Theoretical Fundamentals:

In order to define the issue and explain it completely, it is needed in the following discussion, first the discussions about the basis of the international law should be submitted that the natural law doctrine is of great importance from the view point of the theoretical bases. Nature, wisdom, justice, morality and divine rights are all the concepts which are evolved from the natural law concepts. From the view point of the advocates of natural law doctrine, it is understood that the basis of the laws-generally and international law specifically are put in the metaphysics and it is emphasized that there are general principles and rules which govern the individuals and States and the States have to obey them. In other words, principles and rules are beyond the will. Tomas Habz philosopher and the British jurist only considers natural law as the basis of international law. But from his view point, the most important principle of the natural law is the right of self-preservation (Movahed, 1381, p160).

In the framework of natural law we are faced with a collective of primordial, eternal and immutable rights which do not need the elapse of the time and it includes all the humans from every race and sex. Therefore, no statuary and contractual rule can deprive them of a human. From the view point of those who believe in the common humanistic nature, the inspired rules from the nature of human are so basic that the final aim of a regulation are the rights which are based upon the general awareness and pursuit of human values rules which are the proper finale for the human.

On this basis, the legal regulation which is contained of natural law principles is beyond the desire of the individuals. This point must be mentioned that, the teachings of natural law doctrine specially at the beginning of nineteenth century was weakened, however this fact must not considered as the complete disappearance of principle and beliefs of natural law. In this regard, some has used the expression of the hibernation. Although the natural aw lost its position as an inclusive basis of international law for a while , as we will explain later, form the late nineteenth century we see the reviving its ideas and thoughts in the fundamental field of international law. Generally the basic principles of the law are as old as the State. In the framework of this school unlike natural laws which imagined the legal rules as fixed and eternal and know the State as the positive law of these rules , its advocates know the international law rules as the product of the States will. In this regard, the system which is meant by lawyers is a logically consistent system which creates beyond a deductive pure process, all the rules required for making decisions about the existing and possible issues in the system. Likewise, unlike the natural law attitude in which belief in metaphysical basis was of great validity and merely by induction, the nature of them can be achieved, the positive law can be achieved by induction and without resorting to the principals of metaphysical concepts. (Shahbazi, 2010, p129).

Thus "real law", "ideal law", "law at the same level with reality", " law at the same level of value" are distinct from each other. Such an attitude does not necessarily contradict with the idea which considers "law" as a result of divine will and the nature of the objects or human. However, based on the definition, the laws which are not made of will, are not"law" on their own and it means that they should enter into the positive law to become accessible. In other words, Laws have to be made. Often "positive law" and "natural law" are put against each other (Falsafi, 2008, p22). Although the positive law doctrine has more consistency with the international system because of the consideration of consent and the States' will as the basis of the formation of rules, it could not and also it cannot be responsible of the issues and requirements of the current international community. The development of the human rights and other humanistic considerations especially from the early twentieth century showed the reviving the principles and natural law ideas in the international law area. Specifically ratification and formulation of the Hague Conventions of 1899 and 1907, the adoption of the UN Charter in 1945, that its introduction begins with "we the people of the United States" and the human dignity and fundamental human rights are among the aims and desires of the United Nations. Issuing of the Universal Declaration of Human Rights in 1948, ratification of the Civil and Political Rights in 1996, ratification of the four Geneva Conventions in 1949, ratification of the adjoined Protocols in 1977, the real manifestation of the humanistic values in the form of valuing an individual in the international law by predicting individual complaints in international juridical institutions.

Special attention of the International Court of Justice to the humanistic aims and desires, drafting and ratification of the binding Genocide convention in 1948 and the ratification of several human rights' documents…, and also the dimensions of the permanent and temporary inter States criminal courts in order to act against the serious and systematic violations of the humanistic values. In this framework we can name the establishment of the Nuremberg and Tokyo Criminal tribunals, Criminal Court for the former Yugoslavia and Rwanda and the International Criminal Court in 2002, and it should be noted that not paying attention to the power and the role of the accused official during the prosecution and punishment is another great traits of the above courts), the establishment of several judicial and quasi-judicial institutions especially in the area, all shows the importance of the principles and basis of the natural laws in the international level. Nowadays, human right is another saying of the natural law.

The existence and the validity of the human right is not because of the States' will, It appears that the current system is under the influence of some transitions such as development of the humanistic concept and initial humanistic considerations. In some fields we can adjust the role of States' will and its direct influence in the positive law. In other words, it's the replacement of the bases and votes of the natural law instead of the States' will in the process of creating international positive law rules. This issue has been discussed in the beginning of this discussion. As highlighted above, the ratification of the Martens clause can be a criterion for the acceptance of the mentioned transition and the recognition of the number 3 article common to the four Geneva conventions which are the reflection of this clause, was on this basis and in this framework of the International Court of Justice -in Nicaragua case-.

In addition, the International Criminal Court for the former Yugoslavia has explicitly announced that, since in the current time the imagination of a customary law creation with relying on the consistent and adjusted States (the material element of custom) is nearly impossible. Due to the Martens clause, the principles of the international humanitarian law can emerge as a citation and resort to the humanistic clauses (Opinio Juris)[1]. And in this regard, professor Meron have also acknowledged that the Martens clause has strengthen an attitude on the basis of which the process of the formation of the customary international law, is at first as the basis of the State practice.(Meron,2000.p88) Also professor's kassese attitude toward this clause was the same(Kassese,2000,p241). "what is Martens clause?" This clause was first stated in order to solve the problem among the members of the Hague peace conference on the position of the resistance movements in the occupied territories. The States thinking that the inhabitant of the occupied territories who have weapons should be regarded as legitimate combatants, could not gain the majority vote for

---

1. ICTY. *Kupreskic Case,* Judgment, 14 January 2000, Para 527.

their proposal. And because of this, the regulations related to the position of the combatants in the articles 1 and 2 of Hague Regulations, did not put the resistant forces' combatants among the list of the combatants. Most of the States considered the Martens clause as a suggestion; on the basis that the article 1 and 2 should not be treated as the last sayings about the combatant's legal situation and the issue that whether the combatants of the resistance force have the same situation or not, should not merely determined through the mentioning of omitting them. But we should solve this by this principle" in cases which are not included in this treaty or other international agreements, the military and non-militaries should remain under the support and authority of the international law principles which are as a result of certain practices and humanity principles"

But nowadays the Martens clause in relation to the all territory of humanistic rights, is trustworthy and this can be approved and acknowledged in most of the documents. (Mosaed, 1387, p55). The Martens Clause was first submitted by professor Fredrich van Martens from Livonia of Russian Empire in The Hague Peace convention. And it is written in the introduction of the 1899 and 1907 conventions." Until a more complete code of the law is issued, High Contracting Parties think it right to declare that in cases not included in the Regulations adopted by them, populations and belligerents remain under the protection and empire of the principles of international law, as they result from the usages established between civilized nations, from the laws of humanity, and the requirements of the public conscience."Professor Martens believes that the content of this clause has a historical root and it has its roots in the ideas of natural law. (Meron, 2000, p70)

The point which forms the basis of this discussion and we have discussed about that greatly. Although this announcement in today's world is the inheritance of the Hague Peace conventions in the late nineteenth century, it does not mean that its basis is limited to that period and about a specific issue. The basis and the framework of this clause were always of great importance and citation and as previously mentioned nowadays, it is more trustworthy in comparison to the humanistic law territory. Judicial procedure of the Nuremberg tribunal, the act of International Court of Justice, the activities of the human rights organizations and several documents and treaties related to The Four Geneva conventions (Article 69 of the first convention, article 62 of the second convention, article 142 of the third convention, article 158 of the fourth convention) and the adjoined protocols in 1977 (article 1 (2) of the first protocol and paragraph 4 introduction of the second protocol).

All show the globally acceptance and the general acceptance of the Martens Clause at international level. The principles which are mentioned as the principle of humanity and the conscience principle mentioned in the Martens Clause, make the framework of the human rights system and a part of general common belief of the world (Opinio Juris)[1] that no State can ignore it. In other words, believing in the humanity principles and humanistic considerations especially at present is part of basic, common values of the international community and if a State does not pay attention to them, undoubtedly it cannot have a position in today's international community[2].

---

1. Case concerning Legality of the Threat or Use of Nuclear Weapons, op. cit., *Dissenting Opinion of Judge Weeramantry, p.490, also see: Meron, T, The Martens Clause, Principles of Humanity, and Dictates of Public Conscience*, op. cit., *p.84.*

2. In this regard see: *Millennium Declaration,* United Nations, A/55/1.2, 2000.
Coupland, Robin, *Humanity: What is it and Hon' does it Influence International Law?, 83* International Review of the Red Cross (IRRC), 2001.

3.5.2. The Procedure of the International "Judicial Practice":

From the conceptual and general view point, it was previously mentioned in detail about the modern custom and the process of its recognition in the international judicial practice. Undoubtedly, nowadays, the dominant procedure in the process of the recognition of the customary rules related to the humanistic considerations is affected by the transitions which result from the development of the related concepts. It is transited from the initial recognition to the central discovery of "legal belief".If we put apart the theoretical basis of this transition, it should be noted that it is necessary to investigate the procedures of some valid international judicial organizations. It is obvious that just a collection of the judicial ideas in order to introduce the procedure, is enough.

3.5.2.1. International Court of Justice:

As previously mentioned, the recognition of the article 3 common to the Four Geneva conventions in 1949 by the international court of justice in the case of Nicaragua was a turning point in the new international judicial practice in the recognition process of the customary international law. In the case of armed conflict not of an international character occurring in the territory of one of the High Contracting Parties, each Party to the conflict shall be bound to apply, as a minimum, the following provisions:

(1) Persons taking no active part in the hostilities, including members of armed forces who have laid down their arms and those placed ' hors de combat ' by sickness, wounds, detention, or any other cause, shall in all circumstances be treated humanely, without any adverse distinction founded on race, color, religion

or faith, sex, birth or wealth, or any other similar criteria. To this end, the following acts are and shall remain prohibited at any time and in any place whatsoever with respect to the above-mentioned persons:(a) violence to life and person, in particular murder of all kinds, mutilation, cruel treatment and torture;(b) taking of hostages;(c) outrages upon personal dignity, in particular humiliating and degrading treatment (d) the passing of sentences and the carrying out of executions without previous judgment pronounced by a regularly constituted court, affording all the judicial guarantees which are recognized as indispensable by civilized peoples.

(2) The wounded and sick shall be collected and cared for. An impartial humanitarian body, such as the International Committee of the Red Cross, may offer its services to the Parties to the conflict. The Parties to the conflict should further endeavor to bring into force, by means of special agreements, all or part of the other provisions of the present Convention. The application of the preceding provisions shall not affect the legal status of the Parties to the conflict. As it was considered, the international law derived from Voluntarism has never fulfilled his goal in maintenance of international peace and security; because based on its contractual approach has made imbalanced world's legal system and consequently the legal mechanisms have lost their capability in realization of justice. For example, with formation of Non-proliferation Treaty created to stop production and proliferation of nuclear weapon based on the principles of Voluntarism, finally led to the production of last generation of atomic weapons for nuclear weapon States and also production of first generation of atomic weapons for non-nuclear States. Moreover, numbers of nuclear threats increased and in my opinion more than anything else, it is rooted in the wrong fundamentals governing on such treaty- which will be discussed in detail within next section-. In

the meantime, the legal regime of nuclear fatwa appears and with a superior status and in position of total defending the human dignity, banns any kind of production, proliferation and stockpiling of nuclear weapons and has this potential to be recognized as an international customary rule; as the harbinger of sustainable peace based on the just processes.

"Nuclear fatwa has a same direction with natural law, and in fact is not creator of any added right to human nature and common conscience of humanity, rather is a confirm for fundamentals of natural law, accordingly has been welcomed internationally. In a more general view, this discussion whether nuclear fatwa can create a customary rule or not, disclose a historical battle between advocates of positivists and natural law; whether is it possible to legislate a rule upper than the general nature and human? Or not, legislation of rules merely have reflexive aspect and reflects the constant legal system of world? The basis of many problems are originated from this fact that when we emphasis on the principle of will sovereignty, on one hand that is the amplifier of international law legislation is remarkable but on the other hand that can make a fertile ground for swerving from realization of natural law, i.e. unlike the humanitarian principles and common conscience of humanity; only because of a will, is really worrying. Therefore, the analysis of nuclear fatwa notably clarifies the scope of conflicts in international law and various doctrines, and also enlightens their actually effects. The controversy is that, international law is not formable only based on propensities, rather it exists spontaneously and with relying on humanitarian principles and common conscience of humanity and it needs to be only discovered and recognised; like rule of gravity that itself was not the creator of gravity but its discoverer.

In this phase the battle between positivists and opponents is boosted. First group believes that the axis of values system is will, whereas the second group believes that the values system exists and is independence from the will. For example, if a value is right, no will can take the legitimacy of that right away but the classic system of the formation of international custom has built his basis based on practice emanating from State will, consequently if a will makes a consensus around the falsehood, naturally is formed an untruth custom that among the naturalist is inherently false, because it is in conflict with determined legal system. According to Reflexism, nuclear fatwa has such an aspect. i e, this decree and regulation is the discoverer of common humanitarian principles and noble human values; not create or negate a right spontaneously.

According to Reflexism, "will" cannot affect the truth, years of years the universal will believed that solar system is earth-based and executed whoever disbelieved in it, whereas the truth was the other thing and never was affected by the collective will. When there is no any will for acceptance or rejection of a truth or value, is not effective in its legitimacy and existence. For example, imagine a specialist surgeon who his abilities are undeniable but people do not see him for treatment, in fact there is no any collective will on his specialty; now, can this lack void her specialty as a surgeon? The response is absolutely negative, therefore, a will cannot affect the truth. The other fundamental question here is that; has the current international law system that more than anything else has been built based on Voluntarism -and State will plays a major role in its realization- reached his ultimate goals or not? What seems to be correct is that, those sorts of wills are important that are consistent with truth and at least are not in contrast with human and moral system and heritage of common conscience of humanity. Hence, the ideal system of international law is a system that accepts natural law perfectly and positivism and will-based values system conditionally." (Seivanizad, 2013, p 38)

3.6. Comparative Study of Fatwa Sui Generis with N.P.T and the Advisory Opinion of International Court of Justice:

3.6.1. Generalities:

"The nuclear weapons non-proliferation and disarmament principles are stated within the legal framework of the NPT. The NPT is largely the result of proliferation concerns mainly of the nuclear weapon States, that is, concerns about the dangers of nuclear weapons proliferation, as well as seeking to keep their monopoly on the possession of nuclear weapons. After long and arduous negotiations, the treaty, composed of an introduction and 11 articles, was concluded and signed in 1968, and entered into force in 1970. The NPT has resulted from a compromise between two contending priorities, non-proliferation of nuclear weapons, on one hand, and the use of nuclear energy for peaceful purposes, on the other.

The Treaty is based on three pillars: non-proliferation of nuclear weapons; the right of States to nuclear energy for peaceful purposes; and finally, nuclear weapons disarmament. We would refer to these as international principles on nuclear weapons non-proliferation and disarmament. In a clearly discriminatory fashion, the NPT has divided the States into nuclear-weapon and non-nuclear-weapon States, with different rights and responsibilities. Through specific means and procedures, non-nuclear-weapon States are prohibited from acquiring the weapons. In contrast, however, no specific procedures or plans are envisaged for nuclear weapons disarmament. Articles one and two are related to the nuclear non-proliferation principle. Non-nuclear-weapon States undertake to refrain from acquiring nuclear weapons, and nuclear-weapon States undertake not to transfer the weapons to others. Article three refers to safeguards procedures to verify compliance with non-diversion of nuclear materials from peaceful uses to weapons purposes. Each non-nuclear-weapon State Party to the Treaty undertakes to accept safeguards, as set forth in an agreement to be negotiated and concluded with the International Atomic Energy Agency (IAEA) in accordance with the Statute of the IAEA and the Agency's safeguards system, for the exclusive purpose of verification of the fulfillment of its obligations assumed under this Treaty with a view to preventing diversion of nuclear energy from peaceful uses to nuclear weapons or other nuclear explosive devices[1].

Articles 3, 4 and 5 relate to "the inalienable right of all the Parties to the Treaty to develop research, production and use of nuclear energy for peaceful purposes"[2]. Disarmament of nuclear weapons principle is contained in NPT Article VI. Each of the Parties to the Treaty undertakes to pursue negotiations in good faith on effective measures relating to cessation of the nuclear arms race at an early date and to nuclear disarmament, and on a treaty on general and complete disarmament under strict and effective international control[3]. The Treaty provides for the possibility of withdrawing from it under certain conditions: Each Party shall in exercising its national sovereignty have the right to withdraw from the Treaty if it decides that extraordinary events, related to the subject matter of this Treaty, have jeopardized the supreme interests of its country. It shall give notice of such withdrawal to all other Parties to the Treaty and to the United Nations Security Council three months in advance. Such notice shall include a statement of the extraordinary events it regards as having jeopardized its supreme interests. The article also deals with the duration of the Treaty. "Twenty-five years after the entry

---

1. NPT Article III.1.
2. Commentary part. NPT Article IV.
3. Commentary part. NPT Article X.1.

into force of the Treaty, a conference shall be convened to decide whether the Treaty shall continue in force indefinitely, or shall be extended for an additional fixed period or periods.[1]"

3.6.2. Compatibility of the Edict's Legal Regime with N.P.T Master Keys

Although, the Fatwa's legal undertaking is of a unilateral character, and that of the NPT is an international one, there are important legal similarities and differences between the two. It is realized that: Although often welcome, unilateral initiatives have limitations. Some of them have not been verified, are not subject to any transparency or reporting requirements, are readily reversible, or are not legally binding. Retiring obsolete weapons while developing replacements cannot be seen as a fulfillment of a commitment to disarm. (WMD Commission, 2006: 44)

Similar to the NPT, although no specific verification mechanism of its own is envisaged in the Fatwa, a clear reference to Iran having placed "the entire scope of its nuclear activities under IAEA safeguards and the additional protocol in addition to undertaking voluntary transparency measures "has officially been made in relation to the Fatwa (IAEA, 2005: 121). Also, as argued in a previous section, the anti-WMD commitment made in the Fatwa is not reversible and is legally binding. Contrary to that, NPT Article 10 allows for reversal of the commitment, that is, a State's withdrawal from the treaty. Finally, with respect to developing replacements, it is important to realize that, while the NPT bans a specific type of weapon, nuclear weapons, the Fatwa's prohibition covers all sorts of WMD, even those that could be invented and developed in the future. Therefore, somehow in contrast to the above WMD Commission's suggestion, the Fatwa's unilateral nature has not made it more limited than the NPT, which is a

---

1. Purview. NPT Article X.2.

multilateral international treaty.

In general, both the Fatwa and the NPT have legal implications on Iran, prohibiting the latter from the acquisition, production, stockpiling and use of nuclear weapons. However, the Fatwa, covering all sorts of WMD, including nuclear, chemical, biological, and radiological weapons, and any future weapons or methods of warfare which are indiscriminate in their effect, go far beyond the restrictions set by the NPT, which only concerns nuclear weapons. According to the Fatwa, WMD are canonically wrong and sinful, and from the governance view point, prohibited and illegal. In this manner, the legal prohibition set by the Fatwa is deeply rooted in the religious and moral values of the Iranian people. Therefore, Iran's commitment made through the Fatwa is much more than a government's legal undertaking in respect of an international treaty. Iran's deep rooted religious and moral commitment through the Fatwa adds to the stability and long lasting character of the commitment made through the NPT. Specifically, NPT articles one and two are related to the nuclear non-proliferation principle. Non-nuclear-weapon States undertake to refrain from acquiring nuclear weapons, and nuclear-weapon States undertake not to transfer the weapons to others. Although worded somehow differently to the NPT, the Fatwa restricts Iran in ways no less restrictive than the NPT. For instance, NPT Article 2 refers to terms such as "non-acceptance of transfer", "explosive devices", "not to seek or receive any assistance in the manufacture of nuclear weapons". Although, the Fatwa does not make use of these terms, it clearly and strongly bans nuclear weapons, effectively covering the concerns raised in Article 2.

NPT Article 3(1) refers to safeguards procedures to verify compliance with non-diversion of nuclear materials from peaceful uses to weapons purposes. Similarly, although no specific verification mechanism of its own is envisaged in the Fatwa, a clear reference to Iran having placed "the entire scope of its nuclear activities under IAEA safeguards and the additional protocol in addition to undertaking voluntary transparency measures" has officially been made in relation to the Fatwa (IAEA, 2005: 121). To be agreed by each non-nuclear weapon State with the IAEA, the Additional Protocol is a supplement to any existing comprehensive safeguards agreement between a State and the IAEA. Therefore, in addition to the IAEA safeguards referred to in the NPT, the Fatwa is also cognizant of the Additional Protocol, which required, among other things, a State's further legal authority for a considerably more effective IAEA inspection of any suspect nuclear activities.

An issue of key importance, reflected in NPT Articles 3, 4 and 5, relate to "the inalienable right of all the Parties to the Treaty to develop research, production and use of nuclear energy for peaceful purposes without discrimination". As related to the conduct of the safeguards, NPT Article 3(3) specifically points out that they "shall be implemented in a manner ... to avoid hampering the economic or technological development of the Parties or international co-operation in the field of peaceful nuclear activities". Basically with the same considerations, the issue is also of key importance to the Fatwa. However, in this context, the fundamental matter of the State's national independence is much more explicitly referred to by the Fatwa (Khamenei, 2004). Since the NPT's genesis, there has been a give-and-take between the right to peaceful uses and the non-proliferation commitment. The Fatwa, however, there has never been any indications, whatsoever, of conditionality between the WMD-ban and the right to peaceful nuclear energy. While the Fatwa has unilaterally and unconditionally banned WMD, in the NPT no specific procedures or plans are envisaged for nuclear weapons disarmament. Worse than that is the NPT wording on the issue, connecting negotiations on nuclear disarmament with the "cessation of the nuclear arms race at an early date", on one hand, and "a treaty on general and complete disarmament", on the other hand, rendering the nuclear disarmament as a far-fetched dream. Thus, in this respect, too, the Fatwa stands at a higher moral and legal ground than the NPT. The Treaty provides the right to a State party to withdraw from it "if it decides that extraordinary events, related to the subject matter of this Treaty, have jeopardized the supreme interests of its country"[1]. In clear contrast to the Treaty, according to the Fatwa, regardless of all conditions, including supreme national interests of Iran being in jeopardy, there is no withdrawing from the WMD-ban.

Finally, regarding the Treaty's duration, following an agreement made in a NPT Conference, in 1995, it was decided that the Treaty will continue in force indefinitely. However, considering that the agreement, including commitment to nuclear disarmament, necessity for the universalization of the NPT, and establishment of a nuclear weapons free-zone in the Middle East, is not being honored by nuclear-weapon-States, the indefinite duration of the Treaty is increasingly at risk. In comparison, the Fatwa's duration, not being subject to multilateral agreements or situations, but instead, based on deep-rooted Islamic teachings and moral tenets, is permanent"[2].

3.6.3. The Superiority of Fatwa to the System of Treaties

Can Supreme Leader's fatwa be a performance bond in non- (production, use and stockpiling) of WMD for Iran or not? If this fatwa has a performance bond, is its credibility stronger or weaker than N.P.T?

---

1. Expiry. NPT Article X.1.
2. Even though the writer had written a comprehensive comment, because of better explanation by the article of Iran's Nuclear Fatwa written by Dr. Sirjani, it was directly reflected here.

Based on the applicable Islamic rules in Iran, when *Valliye Faqih* issues a fatwa that enjoys the primary State order status, obeying it, is indispensable for all. Therefore the performance bond of fatwa is undeniable but whether which one stronger performance bond has, some points must be posed here.

I).

Based on this Quranic principle that states: "O people who have believed (in God) fulfil your obligations"[1] Treaties and all agreements are binding for Muslims. And Islamic States, by signing a treaty, in addition to the legal and moral commitment, are committed also religiously. Hence the commitment evolved from fatwa is inviolable.

II).

In spite of the first point, the contracts and treaties are a kind of agreement and as a result of the commitment between human and human, but fatwa is the commitment of human in front of God, that is naturally more important for Muslims.

III).

The components of a treaty is composed of human will, that is formed after the negotiations by full-power representatives, and finally is ratified in a specific form. In Iran, for instance, the international treaties must be ratified by the parliament[2] and then will be recognized as an applicable rule. But the components of fatwa is not composed of human will and derived from the God will which has been extracted from the sources such as: Quran, Narrations, Consensus and Reason. Therefore, base of fatwa is divine and base of a treaty is man-made.

IV).

---

1. "يا ايها الذين آمنوا اوفوا بالعقود..." Quran, the Sura of ALmaedeh, verse 1;
2. The principle 77 of Iran's Constitution

Treaties are reserveable. "Reservation" is a well-known principle in realm of international law of treaties. According to this principle, at the acceptance time of a treaty, States have the right of reservation, i.e. in case of conflict between an article of treaty with domestic law, domestic law will have superiority. But there is no such a thing under the legal regime of fatwa. Nobody has the right of reservation in religious affairs and cannot exclude himself from the inclusion circle of fatwa.

V).

International treaties are revocable, and based on an expediency, some contents of a treaty may be breached, but fatwa does not have such a nature. When something has been religiously prohibited, that prohibition is not changeable, even because of an expediency. For example, production of WMD, because of the expediency of preemption in defending the country borders, is not justifiable under the fatwa regime. It must be emphasized that the aforementioned fatwa, based on the obvious decisive Islamic reasons, i.e. inconsistency of WMD with the Islamic principle of retaliation set forth in some Quranic verses, is not revocable[1].

VI).

International treaties have duration and are terminable. For example, in early Islam in case of "*Hodaibiyyeh*[2]" conciliation, we know that the treaty between Prophet and atheists was concluded for ten years (however, this treaty was breached by atheists before ten years). International treaties also can be concluded with specific duration, but fatwa does not obey this practice, and its content is permanently feasible. Therefore, that is a misconception if we believe that it's possible to issue a fatwa in prohibition of WMD

---

1. Quran, Sura of Anfal, verse 60, "واعِدّوا لهم مااستطعتم من قوه و من رباط الخيل...".
2. The temporary (10 years) ceasefire agreement between Muslims and Atheists.

just for five or ten years.

VII).

One of the legal issues that always has been the fundamental component of the legal regulations is the performance bond of a rule and prosecuting judicial authority in case of its breach. Under international treaty system, in case of treaty breach by a State member party, it will be charged to something that has been previously agreed and specified in the body of treaty. But according to nuclear fatwa issued by Valiye Faqih, in case of its breach by any person, in addition of being a public crime before the law, as well is a major sin before God. Consequently the performance bond of fatwa is stronger than a treaty; because enjoys both binding religious and legal aspects.

VIII).

Some treaties mostly create rights. For example the State member of Non-Proliferation Treaty has the right to have peaceful nuclear technology. The right is basically dispensable, whereas the fatwa, along with the right, creates the obligations, and obligation is not dispensable at least by the promiser. Therefore, any conclusion of an agreement or contract obligate I.R.I to certain commitments. But that is logical and predictable, the States that breached their commitments repeatedly, to be worrier of happening it by others and subsequently underestimate the performance bond that has been determined by themselves and as well United Nation's mechanisms. Nevertheless, after the historical issuance of the nuclear fatwa, IRI was rationally presented a serious and inviolable performance bond to the world.

3.6.4. The Legality of Threat or Use of Nuclear Weapons:

Perhaps when the project of asking ICJ in1992 was posed, no one imagined that the end of this goes contrary to the general belief. Apparently, the benevolent thoughts and peaceful motives made by the presenters of this project- non-governmental[1] organization- was the harbinger of the formation of a movement that, with cooperation of States, was about to lead into a good result in the world. But the court's opinion was not in this regard. If there was a little doubt about the non-strength of theories relating to the legality of use, or the threat of nuclear weapons, from 1996 onwards, not only such doubts have been increased, but also they have been legally consolidated and cited to ICJ related deduction. Hence, some cynical perceptions from the backstage of NGOs pressure, in order to refer this question to ICJ, do not seem to be unfounded. Before the issuance of ICJ advisory opinion concerning the legality of use or threat of nuclear weapon in 1996, almost all international jurists unanimously believed that the use and threat of nuclear weapons is illegal. But after the issuance of this opinion, the aforementioned general consensus was eliminated and this matter was finally considered in favor of the nuclear powers.

In 14 December of 1994, the general secretary of the United Nations formally sent the decision of the general assembly on requesting for the advisory opinion of this judicial organ. In the framework of this request, the general assembly, with the consideration of States commitment in connection with refraining from the threat or the use of force against the territorial integrity or political independence of each other, and also with recalling its resolutions 1653 of 24 November 1961,33/71 b of 14 December 1981, 34/83 G of 11 December of 1979, 35/152 D of 12 December of 1980 and 36/92 I of 9 December of 1981, in which the use of nuclear arms had been recognized as the breach of UN

---

1. Including the International Peace Bureau in Geneva, International Population for Prevention of Nuclear War, International Association of Lawyers Against Nuclear Arms, International Organization Of Greenpeace and so on.

Charter and crime against humanity, required ICJ for his opinion whether the threat or use of nuclear weapons in all circumstances before the international law is valid or not?[1]

Subsequent to this request, ICJ began several processes of proceedings, and finally in 8 July of 1996 issued his advisory opinion.[2] Generally ICJ advisory opinion concerning the legality of the threat or use of nuclear weapons is investigable from the various aspects such as the international humanitarian law and analysis of principles like Distinction between Civilians and Combatants, non-imposing unnecessary pain and suffering, international human rights including some provisions of the Covenant of Civil and Political Rights and the Convention against Genocide, and also the law of the use of force in light of the United Nation's Charter.

---

1. Case concerning Legality of the Threat or Use of Nuclear Weapons, op. cit., *paras. 1 -9*

2. It should be noted, before the question referred by United Nations General Assembly, World hygiene Organization based on the resolution 46/40 of its assembly (14 May) requested ICJ for the same question. This organization in his request declared any effective hygiene service in world cannot quench the effects emanating from the use of even a nuclear weapon, and also the best way to control the hygiene and environmental effects derived from the use of nuclear weapon is only the primary prevention. And with regard to WHO concerns in connection with constant threat of hygiene and environment by nuclear weapons, asked ICJ; with regard to its destructive environmental consequences, whether the use of nuclear arms by a State during a war or the other armed conflicts, is resulted to breach of such a State commitment based on international law including WHO Statute, or not? But ICJ did not reply affirmatively in this respect. On the other words, ICJ based on this idea that requesting for ICJ advisory opinion by World Hygiene Organization as above is out of its jurisdiction based on WHO proceedings framework and also second part of the article 96 of UN Charter. Therefore ICJ refrained from issuance of his advisory opinion based on WHO request. (Advisory Opinion of Legality of the Use by A State of Nuclear Weapons in armed Conflict, *ICJ* Reports, 1996)

Furthermore, the implied emphasis of ICJ to the priority of States sovereignty in all circumstances, which was the main basis and the most controversial part of this opinion. In this regard, ICJ at first and before entering the above entries, pays attention to the field of the law of use of force. According to the court, provisions of Charter relating to the threat or use of force in the framework of Article 2 (part2), 51, 42 enjoys the capability of general application in any conflicts regardless of the type of used armaments, hence, it does not warrant neither the permission nor prohibition of any type of weapons, including nuclear weapon.[1]

Then the Court considers the twofold conditions of "necessity" and "proportionality" in self-defense as the unavoidable principles, regardless of the use of any type of tools and war weapons. And in connection with part four of Article 2 declares; only having nuclear armaments will not make an illegal threat in use of force contrary to these provisions, unless the resort to force is against the territorial integrity or political independence of States, or in contrast with purposes of the United Nations (ibid). Therefore, the Court cannot find a clear response to the legality of resort to nuclear weapons, however this is not considered illegal only by having such weapons. But out of this framework, is there any specific rule under international law relating to inherent legality or illegality of resorting to nuclear weapons? In this phase, the Court investigates a respond to the above question in the field of general international law. The Court, at first, through hinting to this fact that there is no any specific rule prescribing the threat or use of nuclear weapons or any other type of weapon in all or certain circumstances, specifically in the application of self-defense under international law, emphasizes nevertheless there is no any principle or regulation depending on the legality of the threat or use of

---

1. Case concerning Legality of the Threat or Use of Nuclear Weapons, op. at., *para.39*.

nuclear weapons, or any other weapon on a specific authorization under the international law.

According to the Court, State practice shows that the illegitimacy of the use of certain weapons as such does not result from an absence of authorization but, on the contrary, is created[1] in terms of prohibition[2]. The Court, before looking for a specific prohibition in connection with resorting on nuclear weapons in States practice, also considered whether such a prohibition can be found under the international contractual law or not. In this regard, the Court states that the certain provisions of the Second Hague Declaration of 1899, the Regulations annexed to The Hague Convention IV of 1907 or the 1925 Geneva Protocol that has been cited by some States, do not prohibit resorting to weapons of mass destruction (ibid). According to the Court, the consensus built concerning WMD lies in their illegality through some specific instruments.

But the Court does not find any specific prohibition of recourse to nuclear weapons in treaties expressly prohibiting the use of certain weapons of mass destruction; and observes in this way that, although, in the last two decades, many negotiations have been conducted regarding nuclear weapons, they have not

---

1. *Case* concerning Legality of the Threat or Use of Nuclear Weapons, op. cit., *para.52*.

2. It seems that the core of all controversial issues resulting from the Court opinion is formed here. A legitimate point that has been inspired by the State-oriented views of International Court of Justice opinion in lutos case is accepted. The point that had been cited by some States, i.e. what is not prohibited under international law is permitted. It means, the clear prohibition will illegalize some weapons. This type of reasoning by the Court that based on a change in general assembly question- from "prescription" to "prohibition" posed, is really dangerous as it may legitimize use of any new weapon in case of non-clear customary or contractual prohibition.

resulted in a treaty of general prohibition of the same kind for bacteriological and chemical weapons. The Court notes that the treaties dealing exclusively with acquisition, manufacture, possession, deployment and testing the nuclear weapons, without specifically addressing their threat or use, certainly point to an increasing concern in the international community with these weapons. ICJ finally concludes that these treaties could therefore be seen as the landscape of the future general prohibition on use of such weapons, but the mentioned treaties per se do not constitute the world prohibition on WMD - spesifically as the subject of international law-.

Therefore, it seems that the international law has encounter a contradictory situation, on one hand is maintenance claimant of international peace, and on the other does not prescribe any certainty on prohibition of the most destructive weapon of the world. Obviously, getting away from the fundamentals of natural law that was once the basis of international law and also being assimilated into the legal system originated from voluntarism, will be absolutely along with such contradictions. On the contrary, the legal regime of fatwa, because of the origination from the progressive moral principles, and also the dictation of the common conscience, manifested his certainty on illegality of weapons of mass destruction, and does not let this certainty to be affected by any condition.

3.6.5. Conclusions

Issuance of the nuclear fatwa by grand Ayatollah Khamenei is considered as a turning point in the history of the international law. From some aspects, this event is remarkable. First, the issuance of nuclear fatwa happened at the time that Iran was the target of unjust nuclear threats, as its international opponents, namely USA, always were using the language stating "all options are on the desk".

For more than two decades Israel constantly continued to pose nuclear threats against Iran, and in such a situation that all States put the retaliation policy in their agenda, suddenly a massage was transmitted from Iran that could attract everybody's attention in the world, insofar as the hostile States also praised it inevitably. That happened when a Fatwa in prohibition of any production, utilization and stockpiling of WMD was issued. But the Issuance of the fatwa was never surprising for the acquaintances with noble monotheistic ideas.

Because in the not too long time, (about 20 years) when the Iranian territory was slaughtered by foreigners and hundreds of innocent civilians gave up to ghost by enemy's chemical weapons, everyone was awaiting for Iran's decisive response, surprisingly the fatwa in prohibition of production and utilization of WMD from Imam Khomeini's office was transmitted. However, the question remains that what such similar approaches result from? Is not it anything other than complying with a single set of instructions which are the divine teachings of Islam?

The nature of Nuclear Fatwa can be regarded as the demonstration of Iran's commitment to international acts concerning the proscribing WMD and the obligations derived from them. Since the early 20th century, Iran has manifested his propensity to almost all approaches which condemn the use of nuclear, microbial and unconventional weapons including the Hague Conventions, the 1899 Hague Declaration (IV, 2) (concerning Asphyxiating Gases), the 1925 Geneva Protocol for the Prohibition of the Use in War of Asphyxiating, Poisonous or other gases, and of Bacteriological Methods of Warfare, the 1972 Biological and Toxic Weapons Convention, and the 1993 Chemical Weapons Convention. Iran was one of the first States in the western Asia that commenced its amicable nuclear activities in 1957. It signed the NPT in 1968 and ratified it in 1970. It also underwrote safeguard instrument with IAEA in 1973 and lengthened it for infinite time. That was happened at the same time with non-joining the countries like Israel to NPT, in the vicinity of Iran.

Since the 80th decade, Iran has energetically participated in the NPT related conferences aiming at consolidating the disarmament machine and consensus achieved by the atomic States. The Resolution suggested by IRI in the 80th decade, in order to realize a Nuclear Weapon Free Zone (NWFZ) in the western Asia, was agreed by General Assembly. Iran condemned the nuclear States, during the 2010 NPT conference, their failing to harmonizing with commitments set forth in the 1995 decisions and the 13 feasible steps approved in 2000. IRI called on the 2010 review conference to scrutinize the accomplishing these steps and decisions and stated support for ground-making and adoption of a convention prohibiting atomic armaments. Islamic Republic also called on the Atomic States to eschew from: probing and proliferation of nuclear armaments, any threat of atomic armament utilization against non-atomic States, updating nuclear weapons and relevant tools, proliferation of nuclear armaments beyond territorial borders, and putting atomic weapons on offensive state. (PrepCom for the NPT Review Conference, 2009) In the 80th decade, Iran proposed the formation of a nuclear-weapons-free zone in the western Asia, supported that year by Egyptian State (Stevens and Tarzi, 2000). The thought of a western Asia as a NWFZ was first reflected in the 1991 UNSC ceasefire instrument that ended the first Persian Gulf conflict.

IRI has joined to the international act for the Prohibition of the Use in War of Asphyxiating, Poisonous or Other Gases, and of Bacteriological Methods of Warfare (1925) in 1929.(23) Having around 50000 chemical armaments immolations from Iran-Iraq conflicts, Iran is the principle victim of chemical armaments. Almost 20 years after Iran-Iraq armed conflict (1980–88), the wounded still have to tolerate the sores created by chemical weapons. While Saddam used poisonous biological gases in battle fields and even in residential places (Dobbs, 2002; Kessler, 2013), ISI, being a Member State of Geneva Protocol of 1925 and loyal to Islamic tenets and humanistic values, eschewed from retaliation in kind. At the time of battle between Iran and Iraq, the supreme leadership, grand Ayatollah Khomeini, numerously stated that it did not retaliate in kind against Saddam's chemically attacks because of the absolute forbiddance on utilizing poison in Islam. Within Paris conference in 1989, Iran opposed to, and blamed the global village for being isolated in front of Iraq's use of unconventional armaments and convinced international community to finalize the Chemical Weapons Convention (CWC). As the Member States of Disarmament pillar, IRI did its best in negotiation process for the finalization of the agreement and the realization of a structure for the forbiddance of Chemical armaments and underwrote the CWC on January 13, 1993, the first day that it was open for signature, and ratified the Convention on November 3, 1997, as the 82d Member State.

IRI joined the treaty on the forbiddance of the proliferation, Production and Stockpiling of Biological and poisonous Weapons in 1972 and ratified it in 1973. Pursuant to this internationally instrument, modernization, acquiring, stockpiling and transfer of biological and poisonous weapons are prohibited except for amicable purposes. Within the review meetings of this Convention, IRI was one of the most responsible Member States attempting to consolidate its substantial fundamentals and supervising procedure. The principle aim of IRI was to explicitly forbid in the heading and Article 1 of the treaty the «Utilization» of bacterial and microbial armaments. In the inauguration of the Fourth meeting, IRI presented his brilliant proposal to alter the BTWC, debating that in its current status it does not include particular stipulation prohibiting the utilization of these brutal armaments and that the Review meeting brings the first chance, following the finalization of the CWC, to address this basically disadvantages. (BWC/CONF.IV/CRP.1, 1996;BWC/CONF.IV/COW/WP.2, 1996) United States manifested the most intense objections against the improving Convention. (Bucht, et al, 2003: 25-29) IRI role has been very effective in arms reduction fields concerning global CBW treaties (Bucht, et al, 2003: 30) and has repeatedly transmitted an evident and consistent approach against chemical and biological armaments. This is a matter both of its religious opposition to indiscriminate weapons and of its internationally legal obligations. IRI membership in the aforesaid triple principle global acts concerning the WMD and its formation commencement of a NWFZ in the western Asia indicate obviously its State approach and legal commitments in this respect. Nuclear fatwa is not but the proclamation and reassertion of these commitments in framework of a unilateral statement by the Supreme Leadership, the head of State, who enjoys the ultimate authority in specifying the principle policies of Iran regarding the defense and national security of the State, in particular the atomic activities which remarkably root in Islamic fundamentals and teachings.

    The teachings that in their tenets introduce human as the subject of the creation world and the best creature, and consider the highest dignities for him. The current order governing on international law, more than any time else, is based on the unjust approaches, whereby in reaching its aims, has been so dysfunctional that in every corner of the world the flames of a war are visible, and innocent people are being killed. But what is the reason for such a situation? In a general view, it can be stated that the wrong fundamentals governing on international law have caused such a situation. The foundation that in its most important disarmament document completely and discriminatingly divides States into two groups; nuclear-weapon States and non-nuclear weapon States.

And finally, the outcome results in the growth of nuclear threats and weapons in a much wider range than ever before. In the meantime, the legal regime derived from the nuclear fatwa, but this time with a totally different fundamentals and we believe with the right approach, without States division, in the light of a single system, prohibited all States from the acquisition, utilization and stockpiling of weapons of mass destruction, and has not been affected by any condition. Undoubtedly, the growing internationally acceptance of new nuclear idea- especially by independent States- has, more than before, paved the way for the fair formation of a comprehensive system prohibiting any resorting to WMD.

From the other aspect, the issuance of the nuclear fatwa by Iran's supreme leader can be in position of the most tangible guarantees indicating Iran's peaceful approach in its nuclear program, because it is religiously a kind of ultimatum for believers of Islam and monotheism. And based on the principles set forth in Iran's Constitution, this is legally recognized as an inflexible rule. Secondly, it has decisive authenticity as an international unilateral act from the perspective of international law, and in a higher horizon, is considered as a basis to form a new customary order under the international law. Therefore, this has provided an original capacity at Iranian Statesmen disposal in the path of Iranian rights restoration especially in the international communities. On this basis, it is recommended that the ministry of foreign affairs of Islamic Republic of Iran, as the custodian of Iran's foreign policy, operationalize the following measures towards the realization of the anti-weapon approach of the nuclear fatwa in the world.

First, the peaceful approach of Iran in its nuclear activities, based on nuclear fatwa, must be comprehensively globalized through sending a message to all States including both hostile and friendly.

Second, the new round of the international talks in connection with nuclear disarmament should be held -this time with the centrality of the operationalization of the nuclear fatwa-. Third, an association with the attendance of major figures of world religious leaders for globalizing the fatwa and its generalization to the other monotheistic religions must be formed. Fourth, relying on regional international organization's capacities -preferably those which are consistent with the approach of nuclear disarmament- including the Organization of Islamic Cooperation, at the first step of custom-making; the efforts in forming a regional custom evolved from the nuclear fatwa sui generis must be dedicated.

3.6.7. Bibliography

1). English Sources

A). Books

Arechaga, E, J, International Law in the Past Third of a Century, 159 Recueil des cours: Collected Courses of The Hague Academy of International Law, 1978.

Bernhardt, R, Custom and Treaty in The Law of the Sea, 205 Recueil des cours: Colleclcd Courses of The Hague Academy of International Law, 1987.

Brownlie, Ian, Principles of Public International Laiv, Oxford University Press, 1998.

Byers, Michael, Custom, Power, and Power of Rules, Cambridge University Press, 1999.

Cassese, A, International Lmv, Oxford University Press, 2001.

Cassese, A, International Law, Oxford University Press, 2end ed, 2005.

Cheng, B, Custom: The Future of General State Practice in a Divided World, The Structure and Process of International Law: Essays in Legal Philosophy Doctrine and Theory. (R.StJ. Macdonald and D.M.Johnston, eds, 1986).

Cheng, B, Studies in International Space Law, Clarendon Press, Oxford, 1997.

Claude Du Pasquier, Introduction a la theorie generate et a la philosophic du Droit, Delachaux etNiestle, Editeurs, Neuchatel, Paris, 1979.

Condorelli, in Cassese, A, and Weilcr, J, H, eds, Change and Stability in International Law- Making, European University, 1988.

Conforti, B, Cours General de droit international public, 212 Recueild Collected Courses of The Hague Academy of International Law, 1988.

D'amato, A, A, The concept of custom in international law, Cornell University Press, London , 1971.

Digest of United States Practice in International Law, (S, J, Cummins and D, P, Stewart, eds), 2002.

Dinstein Yoram, The Interaction Between Customary International Law and Treaties, 3 Recueil des cours: Collected Courses of The Hague Academy of International Law, 2006.

Dupuy, P, M, Vunite de l'ordre juridique international, Res Cours: Collected Courses of The Hague Academy of International Law, 2000.

Encyclopedia of Public International Law, Karl Doehring, States, Vol.10 (ed by Jochen Abr.Frowein) North-Hollaand, Amesterdam. NewYork. Oxford, 1984.

Fitzmauricc, G, The General Principles of International Law Considered from the Standpoint of the rule of Law, 92 Recueil des cours: Collected Courses of The Hague Academy of

International Law, 1957.

Fitzmaurice, M, Actors and Factors in the Treaty-Making Process, Contemporary Issues in the Law of Treaties, pp.49, 57-58, by Fitzmaurice, M, and Elias, 0, eds, 2005. Brierly, J, L, The Law of Nations, Oxford, 1963.

Freeman, M, D, A, Lloyd's Introduction to Jurisprudence, Sweet and Maxwell, London, 2007.

G.I.A.D. Draper, The Geneva Convention of1949, 114 Recueil des cours: Collected

Gross, L, Essays on International Law and Organization, Two Vols, Martinus Nijhoff, 1984.

Grotius, Hugo, On the Law of War and Peace, Translated from the orginal latin de jure Belli ac Pacis, by A, C, Campbell, Batoche Books, Kitchner, Canada, 2001.

Guggenheim, P, Contribution a Vhistoire des sources du droit des gens, 94 Recueil des cours: Collected Courses of The Hague Academy of International Law, 1958.

Haggenmacher, La doctrine des deux elements du droit coutumier dans la pratique la Cotir international, 90 Recueil des cours: Collected Courses of The Hague Academy of International Law, 1998.

Hart, H, L, A, The Concept of Law, Oxford University Press, 1961. Hobe, S, The Role of Non-State Actors, in Particular of NGOs, in Non-Contractual Law- Making and the Development of Customary International Law, Developments of International Law in Treaty Making, by Wolfram and Rben, eds, 2005.

ICTY Manual on Developed Practices, Prepared in conjunction with UNICRI as part of a project to preserve the legacy of the ICTY, Printed in Turin, Italy, 2009.

J, M, Ilenckaerts and L, Doswald-Beck, Customary

International Humanitarian Law, ICRC, J, M, Henckacrts and L, Doswald-Beck, eds, 2005.

Kelsen, H, The Pure Theory of Law, The Regents of University of California, 1970.

Laurence Boisson, Philippe Sands, International law, The International Court of Justict and Nuclear Weapons, Cambridge University Press, 1999.

Lord Mc Nair, The Law of Treaties, Oxford, Clarendon press, 1961.

Mendelson, M, H, The Formation of Customary International Law, 272 Recueil des cours: Collected Courses of The Hague Academy of International Law, 1998.

Meron, T, International Law in the Age of Human Rights: 301 Recueil des cours: Collected Courses of The Hague Academy of International Law, 2003.

Mullerson, The Interplay of Objective and Subjective Elements in Customary Law, In: Wellens, K, (ed), International Lmv: Theory and Practice: Essays in Honour of Eric Suy, Martinus Nijhoff Publishers 1998.

Schachter, O, International Law in Theory and Practice, 178 Recueil des ours: Collected Courses of The Hague Academy of International Law, 1982.

Statement of Principles Applicable to The Formation of General Customary International Law, The International Law Association, Final Report of 69td Cnference, London, 2000.

Strupp, Les Regies du Droit de la Paix, 47 Recueil des cours: Collected Courses of The Hague Academy of International Law, 1934.

The American Law Institute: Restatement (Third) Foreign Relations Law of The United tates, Vol.1, 1987.

Tomuschat, C, International Law: ensuring the survival of mankind on the eve of a new century, 281 Recueil des cours: Collected Courses of The Hague Academy of International Law, 1999.

Tunkin,G, International politics and the creation of norms of international law, Recueil des cours: Collected Courses of The Hague Academy of International Law, 1989.

Virally, M, The Sources of International Law, In: Soreson, M,(ed), Manual of Public International Law, Martin Press, 1968.

Wolfke, Karol, Custom in present internatonal Improvement, Martinus Nijhoff Publishers, Netherlands, 1993.

Zimmermann, Andreas, Tomuschat Christian, Oellers-Frahm Karin, The Statute of the International Court of Justice, A Commentary, Oxford university press, 2006.

B) Articles

Abi-Saab, G, The International Court as a World Court, in: Fifty Years of The Internatio Court of Justice, Essays in Honour of Sir Robert Jennings, edited by: Vaughan Lowe and Malgosia Fitzmuaurice, Cambridge 1996.

Akehurst, M, Custom as a Source of International Law, 47 British Yearbook of International Law, 1974-75.

Arthur M. Weisburd, Customary International Law: The Problem of Treaties, 21 Vanderbilt Journal of Transnational Law, 1988.

Bernhardt, Customary International Law, In: Bernhardt(ed), Encyclopedia of Public International Law, Vol. 1, 1984.

Cassese, A, The Martens Clause: Half a Loaf or Simply Pie in the SIcy?, European

Cheng, B, General Principles of Law As Applied by

International Courts and Tribunals,1953.

D'amato, A, The Concept of Special Custom in International Law, 63 American Journal of International Law, 1969.

Danilenko, The Theory of International Law, 31 German Yearbook Of International Law,1988.

Elizabeth Roberts, Traditional and Modern Approaches to Customary' International Law: A Reconciliation, 95 American Journal of International Law, 2001.

Emmanuel Voyiakis, A theory of customary international law. Electronic copy available at: http://ssrn.com/abstract=895462

Fidler David, Challenging the Classical Concept of Custom, German Yearbook International Law, 1996.

Fitzmaurice, G, The Formation of the Authority of International Law and the Problems of Enforcement, Modern Law Review, no. 19, 1956.

G, Gilbert, Transnational Fugetive Offenders in International Lmv: Extradition and Other Mechanisms, 1998.

Guzman, T, Saving Customary International Law, 27 Michigan Journal of International Law, 2005.

Hoffmann, T, Dr. Opinio Juris and Mr.St ate Practice: The Strange Case of Customary International Humanitarian Lmv, Budapest 2006.

Hudson, Carolyn, Fishery and Economic Zones as Customary International Law, 17 San Diego Law Review, 1980.

Kunz,The Nature of Customary International Law, 47 American Journal of International Law, 1953.

Lauterpacht, H, The function of Law in the International Community, Archan Books, hamden connecticet, 1966.

Lauterpacht, H, The problem of Jurisdictional Immunities of

Foreign State, British Yearbook of   International Law, 1951.

Meron T, The Geneva Conventions as Customary Lmv, 81 American Journal of International Law, 1987.

Norman, G, Trachtman, P, The Customary International Law Game, 99 American Journal of International Law, 2005.

Omar Abasheikh, The Validity of The Persistent Offender Rule in International Law,9 Coventry Law Journal, 2004.

Sivanizad, Jaber, The Atomic Edict in Comparsion with N.P.T, final book of Ardabil conference 2014.

Sivanizad, Jaber, The Nuclear Fatwa and It,s Legal Status, final book of Ardabil conference 2014.

Schachter,0, Entangled Treaty and Custom, Kluwer Academic Publishers, 1989.

Simma, B, Aleston, P, The sources of Human Rights Law: Custom, Jus Cogens, and General Principles, Astralian Yearbook of International Law, 1988-89.

Simon, Chesterman, The spy Who Came in from the Cold War: Intelligence and International Law, 27 Michigan Journal of International Law, 2006.

Sloan, General Assembly Resolution Revisited, 58 British Yearbook of International Law, 1987.

Sorensen,M, Principles de droit international public, 101 , 1934, 1960.

Stein, T, L, The Approach of the Different Drummer: The Principle of the Persistent   Objector in International Law, 26 Harvard International Law Journal, 1985.

Thirlway, H, International Customary Law and Codification, 1972.

Thirl way, H, The Law and Procedure of International Court

Of Justice, British Yearbook of International Law, 1990.

Tunkin, G, Theory of International Law, 1974.

Verdier, P, H, International Relations, State Responsibility and the Problem of Custom, Virginia Journal of International Law, 2002.

Walden, Raphael, M, The Subjective Element in The Formation of Customary International Law, Israel Law Review, VoI.12, No.3, 1977.

Wilson, S, Famous Mobile Statement, American Journal of International Law, Vol.7, 1913.

Wofgang Friedmann, The North Sea Continental Shef Case, A Critique, 64 American Journal of International Law, 1970.

C). Cases

ICJ & PCIJ

Advisory Opinion of Legality of the Use by A State of Nuclear Weapons in armed Conflict, ICJ Reports, 1996.

Advisory Opinion of Legal Consequences of the Construction of A Wall in the Occupied Palestinian Territory, ICJ Reports, 2004.

Advisory Opinion Of Reparation for Injuries Suffered in the Service of the United Nations, ICJ Reports, 1949.

Advisory Opinion of Reservations to the Convention on the Preventtion and Punishment of the Crime of Genocide, ICJ Reports, 1951.

Advisory Opinion of Western Sahra, ICJ Reports, 1975.

Aegean Sea Continental Shelf Case (Greece v. Turkey), ICJ Reports, 1978.

Asylum Case (Colombia /Peru), ICJ Reports, 1950.

Case concerning Armed Activities on the Territory of the Congo(Democratic Republic of the Congo v. Uganda), ICJ Reports, 2005.

Case concerning Continental ShelffLibyan Arab Jamahiriy a/ Malta), ICJ Reports, 1985.

Case concerning Delimitation of The Maritime Boundary in The Gulf of Maine Area{Canada/UnitedStates of America), ICJ Reports, 1984.

Case concerning Elettronica Sicula S.p.A.(ELSI)(United States of America v. Italy), ICJReports, 1989.

Case concerning Legality of the Threat or Use of Nuclear Weapons, ICJ Reports, 1996.

Case concerning Military and Paramilitary Activities in and against Nicaragua.Jurisdiction, ICJ Reports, 1984.

Case concerning North Sea Continental Shelf, ICJ Reports. 1969.

Case concerning Rights of United Nations National in Morocco, ICJ Reports, 1952.

Case concerning Territorial and Maritime dispute Between Nicaragua and Honduras in Caribbean Sea, ICJ Reports, 2007.

Case concerning The Land Maritime Boundary Between Cameroon and Nigeria, ICJ Reports, 2002.

Csae concerning Application of the Convention on the prevention and Punishment of the Crime of Genos'ule (Preliminary Objection) (Bosnia and Herzegovina v. Yugoslavia), ICJ Reports, 1996.

Jurisdictional Immunities of the State (Germany v. Italy: Greece intervening), ICJ Reports, 2012.

Questions relating to the Obligation to Prosecute or Extradite

(Belgium v. Senegal), ICJ Reports, 2012, 1959.

Land and Maritime Boundary Between Cameroon and Nigeria Case, Preliminary Objection, ICJ Reports, 1998.

Land, Island and Maritime Frontier Dispute(El Salvador/ Honduras: Nicaragua interventing), ICJ Reports, 1992.

Nuclear Tests Case, ICJ Reports, 1974, (New Zeland/France), and (Australia/France).

AFRICA), ICJ Reports, 1966.

The Corfu Channel Case, ICJ Reports, 1949.

PCIJ, Series A/B, Panevezys-Saldutiskis Railway, No.76, 1939.

Advisory Opinion on Customs Regime between Austria and Germany, PCIJ, series AB, 1931.

European Commission of the Danube Case, PCIJ, series B, No. 14,, 1927.

Lotus Case, PCI J, Scries A, No. 10, 1927.

Kourzof Case, PCIJ, Series A, No.9, 1927.

Advisory Opinion of Nationality Decrees Issued in Tunis and Morocco, PCIJ, Series B,No.4, 1923.

Other Tribunals

ICTR, Akayesu Case, Judgment, 2 September 1998.

ICTR, Akayesu Case, Judgment, 2 September 1998.

ICTY, Blaskic Case, judgment, 3 March 2000.

ICTY, Celebici Case, 1998.

ICTY, Jelisic Case, judgment, 14 December 1999.

ICTY, Karadzic and Meladic Case, Review of The Indictment, 11 July 1996.

ICTY, Kordic Case, Decision on The Joint Defense Motion, 2

March 1999.

ICTY, Kunarac Case, Judgment, 22 February 2001.

ICTY, Kupreskic Case, Judgment, 14 January 2000.

ICTY, Martic Case, Review of The Indictment, 8 March 1996.

ICTY, Tadic Case, Interlocutory Appeal, Separate Opinion of JudgS Abi-Saab, 2 October1995.

ICTY. Blaskic case, 2000.

INA Case, INA Corporation v. Iran, Iran - US CL. Trib, 1985.

Arbitral Awards, 1928.

Italy-United Stated Air Transport Arbitration, International Law Reports, 1965.

Oilfield of Texas Case, Oilfield of Texas Inc v. Iran, Iran - US CL. Trib, 1982.

Petroleum Development (Trucial Coast) Ltd. v. Sheihh of Abu Dhabi, International Law Reports, 1951.

Salem Case (Egypt/USA), United Nations Reports of International Arbitral Awards, 1932.

Sedco Case, Sedco v. Iran, Iran - US CL. Trib, 1986.

Texaco Case, Texaco v. Libya, 53 International Legal Reports, 1977.

Amaco Case, Amaco v. Iran, Iran - US CL. Trib, 1986.

Ambatielos case, 1956, Greece/United kingdom, 1963.

Aminoil Case, Aminoil v. Kuweit, 66 International Legal Reports, 1982.

British property in Spanish morocco case, 1925, British/Spanish, United Nations Report oi International Arbitral Awards, Vol.Ill (UNRIAA), United Nations publication, sales no.1949.

D). Documents

Conference on Security and Co-operation in Europe, Helsinki Final Act, 1975.

Declaration on Principles of International Law concerning Friendly Relations and Cooperation among States in accordance with the Charter of the United Nations, GeneralAssembly resolution 2625(XXV), 1970.

Declaration on the Granting of Independence to Colonial Countries and Peoples, GAResolution 1514(XV), 20 December 1960.

Draft Articles on Responsibility of States for International Wrongful Acts, United Natinos, International Law Commission, fifty- third sessions, 2001.

Geneva Convention on the Law High Sea, 1958, 450 United Nations Treaty Series 82.

International Law Commission, Yearbook of International Law Commission, Vol.2, 1976.

UN Security Council, Resolution 764, 1992.

UN Security Council, Resolution 771, 1992.

UN Security Council, Resolution 780, 1992.

UN Security Council, Resolution 808, 1993.

UN Security Council, Resolution 935, 1994.

UN Security Council, Resolution 955, 1994.

United Nations Convention on the Law of the Sea, 1982, Official Text 62 (United Nations),1997.

Vienna Convention on the Law of Treaties Between States and International

E). Websites

Ayatollah khamenei,s speechs are available in this site: www. Khamenei.ir

An interview with Mr. Seivanizad about nuclear fatwa is available in this site: www.presstv.ir

2). Non English Sources

2.1. Persian

اشتراوس، لئو،۱۳۷۳، **حقوق طبیعی و تاریخ**، ترجمه باقر پرهام، انتشارات آگه.

اداره کل امور فرهنگی و روابط عمومی مجلس شـورای اسلامی، ۱۳۶۴، **صورت مشروح مذاکرات مجلس بررسی نهایی قانون اساسی**، تهران، روابط عمومی مجلس شورای اسلامی.

انجمن ایرانی مطالعات سازمان ملل متحد،۱۳۸۹، **نقش دیوان بین‌المللی دادگستری در تداوم و توسعه حقوق بین‌الملل.** (مجموعه مقالات).

تاجیک، محمدرضا، ۱۳۷۹، **مدیریت بحران**، تهران، انتشارات فرهنگ گفتمان.

تسون، فرناندو،۱۳۸۸، **فلسفه حقوق بین‌الملل**، ترجمه محسن محبی، مؤسسه مطالعات و پژوهشهای حقوقی شهردانش، تهران.

جوادی آملی، عبدالله، ۱۳۸۳، **ولایت فقیه، ولایت فقاهت و عدالت**، قم، مرکز نشر اسراء.

چرنی، جاناتان،۱۳۸۷، **تأثیر رشد و گسترش محاکم و مراجع قضایی بر انسجام سیستم حقوقی، در: حقوق بین‌الملل معاصر (نظریه‌ها و رویه‌ها)**، ترجمه نادر ساعد، انتشارات خرسندی.

ذوالعین، پرویز، ۱۳۸۳، **مبانی حقوق بین‌الملل عمومی**، دفتر مطالعات سیاسی و بین‌المللی.

رابین چرچیل و آلن‌لو، ۱۳۷۷،**حقوق بین‌الملل دریاها**، ترجمه بهمن آقائی، کتابخانه گنج دانش، تهران.

روسو، شارل، ۱۳۴۷، **حقوق بین‌الملل عمومی**، جلد اول، ترجمه محمدعلی حکمت، انتشارات دانشگاه تهران.

ریموند وکس، ۱۳۸۹، **فلسفه حقوق از حقوق طبیعی تا پسامدرنیسم**، ترجمه فاطمه آبیار، نشر رخداد نو.

زمانی، سیدقاسـم،۱۳۸۴، **حقوق سـازمان‌های بین‌المللی؛ شـخصیت، مسـؤولیت، مصونیت**، مؤسسه مطالعات و پژوهشهای حقوقی شهر دانش، تهران.

سـاعد، نادر، ۱۳۸۶، **حقوق بشردوسـتانه و سـلاحهای هسـته‌ای، کمیته ملی حقوق بشردوستانه**، مؤسسه مطالعات و پژوهشهای حقوقی شهر دانش، تهران.

شـهبازی، آرامش، ۱۳۸۸، **حقوق بین‌الملل؛ دیالکتیک ارزش و واقعیت**، مؤسسـه مطالعات و پژوهشهای حقوقی شهردانش، تهران.

صحیفه امام، ۱۳۸۶، تهران، مؤسسه تنظیم و نشر آثار امام خمینی (ره).

ضیائی بیگدلی، محمدرضا و همکاران، ۱۳۸۷،**آراء و نظریات مشورتی دیوان بین‌المللی دادگستری**، جلد اول (۱۹۴۸-۱۹۸۶)، انتشارات دانشگاه علامه طباطبایی.

ضیائی بیگدلی، محمدرضا و همکاران، ۱۳۸۸، **آراء و نظریات مشورتی دیوان بین‌المللی دادگستری**، جلد دوم (۱۹۸۷-۲۰۰۰)، انتشارات دانشگاه علامه طباطبایی.

عبداللهی، محسن، شافع میرشهبیز، ۱۳۸۲، **مصونیت قضایی دولت در حقوق بین‌الملل**، اداره کل پژوهش و اطلاع‌رسانی معاونت حقوقی ریاست جمهوری .

عراقی، عزت‌الله، ۱۳۶۷، **حقوق بین‌الملل کار**، انتشارات دانشگاه تهران.

عنایت، حمید، ۱۳۸۴، **بنیاد فلسفه سیاسی در غرب**، انتشارات زمستان.

فلسفی، هدایت‌الله، ۳۹۰، **صلح جاویدان و حکومت قانون، دیالکتیک همانندی و تفاوت**، فرهنگ نشر نو با همکاری نشر آسیم، تهران .

قاضی شریعت‌پناهی، ابوالفضل، ۱۳۷۲، **حقوق اساسی و نهادهای سیاسی**، تهران: مؤسسه چاپ و انتشارات دانشگاه تهران.

کاتوزیان، ناصر، فلسفه حقوق، ۱۳۸۵، **جلد اول تعریف و ماهیت حقوق**، شرکت سهامی انتشار.

کاتوزیان، ناصر، ۱۳۸۴، **اثبات و دلیل اثبات- قواعد عمومی اثبات، اقرار و سند**، جلد اول، چاپ سوم، بهار .

کاسه، آنتونیو، ۱۳۸۵، **حقوق بین‌الملل**، ترجمه حسین شریفی طرازکوهی، نشر میزان .

کلی، جان، ۱۳۸۸، **تاریخ مختصر تئوری حقوقی در غرب**، ترجمه محمد راسخ، انتشارات طرح نو.

کلییار، کلودآلبر، ۱۳۷۱، **سازمانهای بین‌المللی**، ترجمه و تحقیق از هدایت‌الله فلسفی، نشر فاخته.

کلییار، کلودآلبر، ۱۳۶۸، **نهادهای روابط بین‌الملل**، ترجمه و تحقیق از هدایت‌الله فلسفی، نشرنو.

کمیسیون حقوق بین‌الملل سازمان ملل متحد، ۱۳۸۸، **مسؤولیت بین‌المللی دولت**، ترجمه علیرضا ابراهیم گل، مؤسسه مطالعات و پژوهش‌های حقوقی شهردانش، تهران.

مالوری، فیلیپ، ۱۳۸۳، **اندیشه‌های حقوقی**، ترجمه مرتضی کلانتریان، نشر آگه.

ممتاز، جمشید و همکاران ، ۱۳۸۴، **حقوق بین‌الملل بشردوستانه مخصمات مسلحانه داخلی**، کمیته ملی حقوق بشردوستانه، نشر میزان.

موحد، محمدعلی، ۱۳۸۱، **در هوای حق و عدالت، از حقوق طبیعی تا حقوق بشر**، نشر کارنامه، تهران .

موسی‌زاده، رضا، ۱۳۷۷، **حقوق معاهدات بین‌المللی**، نشر دادگستر .

نصیری، محمد، ۱۳۸۶، **حقوق بین‌الملل خصوصی**، جلد اول و دوم، انتشارات آگاه.

نقیبی مفرد، حسام، ۱۳۸۹، **حکمرانی مطلوب در پرتو جهانی شـدن حقوق بشـر**، مؤسسه مطالعات و پژوهش‌های حقوقی شهردانش، تهران .

والاس، ربـکا، ۱۳۸۷، **حقوق بین‌الملل**، ترجمه و تحقیق سیدقاسم زمانی، مهناز بهراملو، مؤسسه مطالعات و پژوهش‌های حقوقی شهردانش، ویرایش دوم، تهران .

وکیل، امیرساعد، ۱۳۸۳، **حقوق بشر، صلح و امنیت بین‌المللی**، زیرنظر دکتر عباس کدخدایی، انتشارات مجد.

مقالات

بروانلــی، ایــان، ۱۳۶۷، **نظری اجمالی بر حقوق معاهدات**، ترجمه احمــد قطینه، مجله حقوقی دفتر خدمات حقوقی و بین‌المللی ریاست جمهوری، ش ۵.

بیگ‌زاده، ابراهیم، ۱۳۷۳-۱۳۷۴، **تأثیر سازمانهای غیردولتی در شکل‌گیری و اجرای قواعد بین‌المللی**، مجله تحقیقات حقوقی دانشگاه شهید بهشتی، ش ۱۵.

پین، اوژن، ۱۳۷۲-۱۳۷۱، **بشـریت و حقوق بین‌الملل**، ترجمه ابراهیم بیگ‌زاده‌ف مجله حقوقی دفتر خدمات حقوقی و بین‌المللی ریاست جمهوری، ش ۱۶-۱۷.

تونکین، گریگوری، ۱۳۷۳-۷۴، **آیا حقوق بین‌الملل عام، تنها حقوق عرفی است؟**، ترجمه سیدفضل‌الله موسوی، مجله حقوقی دفتر خدمات حقوقی و بین‌المللی ریاست جمهوری، ش ۱۸ و ۱۹.

خالقــی، علــی، ۱۳۸۳، **بلژیک و پایان ده سـال رؤیای صلاحیت جهانی در جرائــم بین‌المللی**، مجله پژوهشهای حقوقی مؤسسه مطالعات و پژوهشهای حقوقی شهر دانش، ش ۶.

رفیعی، کمال، ۱۳۸۰، **حل و فصل اختلافات مرزی بحرین قطر از سوی دیوان بین‌المللی دادگستری**، ماهنامه خلیج فارس و امنیت، ش ۱۰.

رنجبریان، امیرحسـین، ۱۳۸۷، **پویائی حقوق بین‌الملل و پایائی شکنجه**، فصلنامه حقوق مجله دانشکده حقوق و علوم سیاسی دانشگاه تهران، دوره ۳۸، ش ۱، بهار.

رنجبریان، امیرحسـین، ۱۳۸۴، **جایگاه قاعده منع شــکنجه در حقوق بین‌الملل معاصر**، مجله دانشکده حقوق و علوم سیاسی دانشگاه تهران، ش ۷۰، زمستان.

رنجبریان، امیرحسین، ۱۳۸۱، **قانون ۱۹۹۳-۱۹۹۹ بلژیک، رأی ۱۴ فوریه ۲۰۰۲ دیوان بین‌المللی دادگستری، صلاحیت کیفری جهانی در بوته آزمون**، مجله دانشــکده حقوق و علوم سیاســی دانشگاه تهران، ش ۵۸.

زمانی، سیدقاسم، ۱۳۷۵، **حقوق قراردادی و تدوین قواعد عرفی در رویه دیوان بین‌المللی دادگستری با تأکید بر قضیه نیکاراگوئه**، مجله حقوقی دفتر خدمات حقوقی و بین‌المللی ریاست جمهوری، ش ۲۰.

زمانی، سیدقاسم، ۱۳۸۸، **فرایند انسانی شدن حقوق بین‌الملل و چاشهای فراروی آن**، مجموعه مقالات هفته پژوهش در دانشکده حقوق و علوم سیاسی دانشگاه علامه طباطبایی.

شریفی طرازکوهی، حسین، ۱۳۸۳، **درآمدی بر بنیان‌های نظری حقوق بشر**، فصلنامه نامه مفید، شماره ۴۶.

ضیائی بیگدلی، محمدرضا، ۱۳۷۸، **پیوندهای بنیادین عرف و معاهده در حقوق بین‌الملل**، مجله پژوهش حقوق و سیاست، دانشکده حقوق و علوم سیاسی دانشگاه علامه طباطبایی، سال اول شماره ۱، پاییز - زمستان.

ضیائــی بیگدلی، محمدرضا، ۱۳۸۹، **رسـالت دیوان در صیانت از حقوق بین‌الملل، در: نقش دیوان بین‌المللی دادگسـتری در تداوم و توسـعه حقوق بین‌الملل**، انجمن ایرانی مطالعات سازمان ملل متحد، تهران.

عبداللهی، محسـن، ۱۳۸۹، **تبیین و توسـعه حقوق کارگزاران سازمانهای بین‌المللی در رویه دیوان**

بین‌المللی دادگستری، در: نقش دیوان بین‌المللی دادگستری در تداوم و توسعه حقوق بین‌الملل، انجمن مطالعات ایرانی مطالعات سازمان ملل متحد، تهران .

فلسفی، هدایت‌الله، ۱۳۷۵، **جایگاه بشر در حقوق بین‌الملل معاصر**، مجله تحقیقات حقوقی دانشگاه شهیدبهشتی، شماره ۱۸ .

فلسفی، هدایت‌الله، ۱۳۸۷-۱۳۸۶، **رویارویی عقل و واقعیت: مسأله منابع**. سالنامه ایرانی حقوق بین‌الملل و تطبیقی، شماره سوم.

فلسفی، هدایت‌الله، ۱۳۷۱، **شناخت منطقی حقوق بین‌الملل**، مجله تحقیقات حقوقی دانشگاه شهید بهشتی، شماره ۱۰ .

کاسسه، آنتونیو، ۱۳۸۳، **تعقیب کیفری کارگزاران عالی‌رتبه دولت‌ها در دادگاه‌های داخلی به اتهام ارتکاب جرائم بین‌المللی (دعوای کنگو علیه بلژیک در دیوان بین‌المللی دادگستری)**، ترجمه حمیدرضا جاویدزاده، مجله پژوهش‌های حقوقی مؤسسه مطالعات و پژوهش‌های حقوقی شهردانش، شماره ۵.

هنجنی، سیدعلی، ۱۳۷۱، **تحولات پیدایش عرف بین‌المللی**، مجله تحقیقات حقوقی، شماره ۱۱-۱۲ . همایش

سیوانی‌زاد، جابر، ۱۳۹۳، **فتوای هسته‌ای نویدگر صلح پایدار**، همایش دیپلماسی هسته‌ای، تهران، دی‌ماه ۹۳، ص ۱۶.

2.2. Arabic Sources

قرآن

ابن ادریس الشافعی، ابوعبدالله محمد، ۱۴۰۳ق، **کتاب الأم**، دارالفکر للطباعة و النشر و التوزیع، الطبعة الثانیة.

ابن البراج القاضی، ۱۴۰۶ ق، **المهذب**، اشراف؛ جعفر السبحانی، مؤسسة النشر الاسلامی التابعة لجماعة المدرسین بقم المشرفة.

ابن خرم الاندلس، ۶۷۸ق، علی‌بن‌احمدبن‌سعید؛ بی‌تا، المحلی، دارالفکر.

ابن‌عبدالبر القرطبیع ابوعمر یوسف بن عبدالله، ۱۳۸۷ ق، **التمهید**، تحقیق، مصطفی بن احمد العلوی، محمدعبدالکبیر البکری، وزراة عموم الأوقاف و الشؤون الاسلامیة، المغرب.

ابن‌عبدالبر، ۲۰۰۰م، **الاستذکار**، سالم محمدعطا- محمدعلی معرض، دارالکتب العلمیة، بیروت، الطبعة الأولی.

ابوالفتوح رازی، حسین‌بن‌علی، ۱۴۱۰ق، **روض الجنان و روح‌الجنان فی تفسیر القرآن**، بنیاد شهرستانی، انتشارات بیدار، قم، چاپ اول.

ابومخنف، ۱۳۷۸، **مقتل الحسین**، تحقیق شیخ محمدهادی یوسفی غروی، ترجمة علی کرمی، مؤسسة مطبوعاتی دارالکتب

احمدی میانجی، علی، ۱۴۱ق، **الاسیر فی الاسلام**، قم، مؤسسة النشر الاسلامی التابعة لجماعة المدرسین، قم المقدسه، الطبعة الأولی.

أصبهانی، ابونعیم، ۱۴۱۵ق، **مسندابی حنیفة**، تحقیق، نظر محمد الفاریابی، الریاض، مکتبة الکوثر، الطبعة الأولی.

البانى، محمدناصر، ۱۴۰۵ق، **ارواء الغليل**، اشراف، زهير الشاويق، بيروت، المكتب الاسلامى، الطبعة الثانية.

برقى، ابوجعفراحمدبن‌محمدبن‌خالد، ۱۳۷۱ق، **المحاسن**، دارالكتب الاسلامية، قم المقدسة، الطبعة الثانية .

بيهقى، احمدبن‌الحسين، بى‌تا، **السنن الكبرى**، بى‌جا، دارالفكر.

ترمذى، محمدبن‌عيسى، ۱۴۰۳ق، **سنن الترمذى**، تحقيق و تصحيح، عبدالرحمن محمدعثمانى، م، دارالفكر للطباعة و النشر و التوزيع، بيروت، الطبعة الثالثة.

التميمى المغربى، نعمان‌بن محمد، بى‌تا، **دعائم الاسلام**، ج۱، بيروت، المكتب الاسلامى.

ثعلبى نيشابورى، ابواسحاق احمدبن‌ابراهيم، ۱۴۲۲ ق، **الكشف و البيان عن تفسيرالقرآن**، بيروت،داراحياء التراث‌العربى.

حرالعاملى، محمدبن‌الحسن‌بن‌على، ۱۴۰۹ق، **تفصيل وسايل الشيعة الى تحصيل مسائل الشريعة**، قم المقدسه، مؤسسة آل‌البيت الاحياء التراث، الطبعة الاولى.

حلى، العلامة الحسن بن يوسف بن المطهر الأسدى، ۱۴۲۱ق، **تلخيص المرام فى معرفة الأحكام**، المحقق/ المصحح، هادى القبيسى، قم المقدسه، مركز النشر التابع لمكتب الاعلام الاسلامى، الطبعة الأولى.

حلى، العلامة الحسن بن يوسف بن المطهر الأسدى، ۱۳۴۳ق، **منتهى المطلب فى تحقيق المذهب**، المحقق/ المصحح، الشيخ حسين پيشنماز أحرابى، مطبعة الحاج أحمد آغا و محمود آغا، الطبعة الاولى۲۹ .

حلى ابن‌ادريس، ۱۴۱۰ق، **السرائر**، مؤسسة النشر الاسلامى، قم، التابعة لجامعة المدرسين، الطبعة الثانية.

خوئى، سيدابوالقاسم موسوى، ۱۴۱۰ق، **المنهاج الصالحين**، قم‌المقدسه، نشر مدينه العلم.

دارمى، عبدالله بن بهرام، ۱۳۴۹، **سنن الدارمى**، طبع بعناية محمداحمد دهمان، دمشق، مطبعة الحديثه.

راوندى، قطب‌الدين سعيدبن‌هبة‌الله، ۱۴۰۵ق، **فقه القرآن فى شرح آيات الأحكام**، قم، كتابخانة آيت‌الله مرعشى نجفى.

زحيلى، وهبة‌بن مصطفى، ۱۴۱۸ق، **التفسير المنير فى‌العقيدة و الشريعة و المنجه**، بيروت، دارالفكر المعاصر.

زركش، بدرالدين محمدبن بهادربن عبدالله، ۱۴۲۷ق، **الديباج فى توضيح المنهاج**، تحقيق، يحيى مرداد، قم، دارالحديث.

سجستانى، ابن‌الشعت، ۱۴۱۰ق، سنن أبى‌داود، **تحقيق و تعليق**، سعيد محمد العام، بيروت، دارالفكر للطباعة و النشر و التوزيع، الطبعة الأولى.

3.6.8. Appendixes

Pictures & Documents

The following pictures -are only some examples- indicating the direct and indirect support of noted individuals and international officials in anti-arm approach of Iran -specifically nuclear fatwa-. All statements, reactions and even behaviors of international officials done in public including body language has legal meaning and bring the international responsibility for their doers. Therefore, all the States -especially nuclear weapon states- that made a meaningful political connection with Iran, during the so-called Iran phobia age, are truly remarkable under international law. During the aforementioned period, many states in spite of the baseless all-sided pressure against Iranian nation, whereas did not have to be in line with Iran, confirming its anti-arm approach derived from the nuclear fatwa, reconsolidated their bilateral relationships with Iran. This would not happen unless they believe in Iran's peaceful approach in its nuclear activities, and what could be more important than the nuclear fatwa indicating this practice? Expressed desires to the nuclear fatwa universally, doubled the significance of this act, because this act enjoys some aspects which distinguish it from the other acts with the same functions. For example as mentioned, N.P.T is a treaty only about nuclear weapons, whereas fatwa includes all possible sorts of WMD, also N.P.T only focused on non-proliferation, whereas the fatwa covers and prohibits all functions of nuclear weapon including for destruction, policy of prevention and test. Hence the opportunity of globalizing such a different document enjoying such capacities is being operationalized by several States.

The meeting between Supreme leader and General Secretary of United Nations- 2012/08/29

The meeting between Supreme leader and president of Russia (N.W.S)[1] -2007/10/16

1. Nuclear Weapon State.

The meeting between Prime Minister of India (N.W.S) and Supreme Leader-2012/08/29

The meeting between Prime Minister of Pakistan (N.W.S) and Supreme Leader-2014/05/14

The meeting between Supreme Leader and Chairman of the Social Commission of W.H.O

The meeting between Supreme Leader and President of Brazil-2010/05/16

The meeting between Supreme Leader and President of Belarus-2006/11/06

The meeting between Supreme Leader and President of Ecuador-2008/12/07

The meeting between Supreme Leader and President of Azerbaijan-2008/05/09

The meeting between Supreme Leader and King of Amman- 2009/08/04

The meeting between Supreme Leader and President of Armenia- 2009/04/09

The meeting between Supreme Leader and King of Qatar- 2009/11/05

The meeting between Supreme leader and President of Bolivia-2008/09/01

The meeting between Supreme Leader and President of Nicaragua- 2007/06/10

The meeting between Supreme Leader and President of Iraq-2009/02/28

The meeting between Supreme Leader and President of Eritrea-2008/05/20

The meeting between Supreme Leader and Time Chairman of I.A.E.A-2008/01/12

The meeting between Supreme Leader and President of Indonesia-2008/03/11

The meeting between Supreme Leader and President of Guyan-2010/01/21

The meeting between Supreme Leader and President of Moritania-2010/01/26

The meeting between Supreme Leader and president of Algeria-2010/05/17

The meeting between Supreme Leader and President of Tajikestan-2012/08/30

The meeting between the Prime Minister of Turkey and Supreme Leader-2012/05/29

The meeting between Supreme Leader and President of Sri Lanka-2012/08/31

The meeting between Supreme Leader and Chairman of the African Union-2013/08/30

The meeting between Supreme Leader and President of Mongolia -2012/09/01

The meeting between Supreme Leader and President of Senegal-2010/05/16

Meeting Between Supreme Leader and President of Zimbabwe-2012/08/30

Formal support of Chinese State for nuclear fatwa-2013/01/17

Support of Iranian Jewish community for nuclear fatwa-2012/12/09

Support of International Institute for Strategic Studies for nuclear fatwa-2013/10/17

Support of President of the World Security Institute in America for nuclear fatwa-2010/04/21

Support of disarmament General director of the Arab League for nuclear fatwa-2010/05/20

Support of Austrian Ambassador in Iran for nuclear fatwa-2010/05/20

United Nations

A/64/752–S/2010/203

Distr.: General
22 April 2010

Original: English

General Assembly
Sixty-fourth session
Agenda item 96
General and complete disarmament

Security Council
Sixty-fifth year

Identical letters dated 20 April 2010 from the Permanent Representative of the Islamic Republic of Iran to the United Nations addressed to the Secretary-General and the President of the Security Council

I have the honour to transmit herewith the message of His Eminence Ayatollah Seyed Ali Khamenei, the Supreme Leader of the Islamic Republic of Iran, delivered to the International Conference on Nuclear Disarmament and Non-Proliferation (see annex). In his message, the Supreme Leader reiterated the principled position of the Islamic Republic of Iran concerning the prohibition of the use of weapons of mass destruction, including nuclear weapons, and stated: "We consider the use of such weapons as *haram* (religiously forbidden) and believe that it is everyone's duty to make efforts to secure humanity against this great disaster".

The International Conference on Nuclear Disarmament and Non-Proliferation, held in Tehran on 17 and 18 April 2010, was attended by high-level officials and prominent experts from 60 countries as well as representatives of relevant international and regional organizations. The purpose of the Tehran Conference was to exchange views on, and find practical ways to advance, the cause of disarmament and non-proliferation. The Conference, among other things, called for the total elimination of weapons of mass destruction and offered some proposals to achieve the lofty goal of a world free from weapons of mass destruction.

The Tehran Conference is yet another firm indication of the seriousness of Iran's stance with regard to the urgency of international actions in the elimination of all weapons of mass destruction and nuclear arms.

It would be highly appreciated if the present letter and its annex could be circulated as a document of the General Assembly, under agenda item 96, and of the Security Council.

(*Signed*) Mohammad **Khazaee**
Ambassador
Permanent Representative

A/64/752
S/2010/203

Annex to the identical letters dated 20 April 2010 from the Permanent Representative of the Islamic Republic of Iran to the United Nations addressed to the Secretary-General and the President of the Security Council

Message from His Eminence Ayatollah Sayyid Ali Khamenei, Supreme Leader of the Islamic Republic of Iran, to the International Conference on Nuclear Disarmament

Tehran, 17 and 18 April 2010

In the name of God, the Compassionate, the Merciful

I should like to welcome the honourable guests who have gathered here. It is a pleasure for the Islamic Republic of Iran to host the International Conference on Nuclear Disarmament today. I hope that you will make use of this opportunity so that all of humanity may benefit from the enduring and valuable conclusions which you will reach through discussion and consultation.

The study of atoms and nuclear sciences are among humanity's greatest achievements. They can and should be used to serve the well-being of nations throughout the world and the growth and development of all human societies. The applications of nuclear sciences cover a wide range of medical, energy and industrial needs, each of which has considerable importance. For this reason, it can be said that nuclear technology has gained a prominent position in economic life. As industrial, medical and energy needs increase, its importance will continue to grow, and efforts to obtain and use nuclear energy will increase accordingly. Just like other nations of the world, the nations of the Middle East are thirsty for peace, security, and progress, and have the right to secure their economic position and improve the situation of future generations through the use of such technology. One of the probable goals behind the sowing of doubts about the peaceful nuclear programmes of the Islamic Republic of Iran is to prevent the nations of the region from giving serious attention to that natural and valuable right.

The interesting point is that the only nuclear criminal in the world currently falsely claims to be combating the proliferation of nuclear weapons. However, it certainly has not taken any serious measures in this regard, and will never do so. If America's claims that it is combating the proliferation of nuclear weapons were true, would the Zionist regime be able to turn the occupied Palestinian lands into a vast arsenal of nuclear weapons, while refusing to respect the relevant international regulations, especially the Treaty on the Non-Proliferation of Nuclear Weapons?

Unfortunately, although the word "atom" is associated with the progress of human knowledge, it is equally associated with the most appalling event in history, and the greatest genocide and misuse of humanity's scientific achievements. Although, many countries have sought to manufacture and stockpile nuclear weapons — which in itself can be viewed as a prelude to the commission of crimes and has seriously jeopardized global peace — only one Government has thus far committed a nuclear crime. Only the Government of the United States of America attacked the oppressed people of Hiroshima and Nagasaki with atomic bombs, in an unequal and inhumane war.

The detonation of the first nuclear weapons by the United States Government in Hiroshima and Nagasaki created a human disaster of unprecedented proportions, and exposed human security to a great threat. Since that time, the global community has reached a unanimous agreement that such weapons must be completely eliminated. The use of nuclear weapons has resulted not only in large-scale killings and destruction, but also in the indiscriminate massacre of soldiers and civilians, young and old, men and women. Its inhuman effects have transcended political and geographical borders, even inflicting irreparable harm on future generations. The use or even the threat of use of such weapons is therefore a serious violation of the most basic humanitarian principles, and clearly constitutes a war crime.

From a military and security perspective, after certain powers obtained this inhuman weapon, there remained no doubt that victory in a nuclear war would be impossible, and that to engage in such a war would be an irrational and inhuman act. However, despite these obvious ethical, rational, human, and even military realities, the strong and repeated call by the global community for the elimination of such weapons has been ignored by a small number of Governments, which have based their illusory security on global insecurity.

The insistence of these Governments on possessing, accumulating and developing the destructive power of such weapons, which have never served any purpose other than to intimidate, terrorize and create a false sense of security based on mutually assured destruction, has perpetuated the world's nuclear nightmare. Innumerable human and economic resources have been expended in this irrational competition to give the superpowers the imaginary capability to annihilate their rivals, along with the other inhabitants of the planet including themselves, more than ten thousand times over. It is for this reason that the strategy has been known as mutually assured destruction or MAD.

In recent years, a number of Governments that possess nuclear weapons have even gone beyond mutually assured destruction in their dealings with other nuclear powers: in their nuclear policies, they insist on maintaining the nuclear option even if they are faced with conventional threats from countries that violate the Non-Proliferation Treaty. At the same time, the greatest violators of the Treaty are the powers that have reneged on their commitment to nuclear disarmament in accordance with Article VI of the Treaty. These powers have even surpassed other countries in promoting the vertical and horizontal proliferation of nuclear weapons around the world. By providing the Zionist regime with nuclear weapons and supporting its policies, these powers are contributing directly and actively to the proliferation of nuclear weapons, thereby contravening their commitments under Article I of the Treaty. These countries, headed by the bullying and aggressive United States regime, pose a serious threat to the Middle East region and the world.

It is incumbent upon for the International Conference on Nuclear Disarmament to investigate the threats posed by the production and stockpiling of nuclear weapons in the world and to propose realistic solutions to counter this threat to humanity. Such action would make it possible to take effective steps towards safeguarding peace and stability.

We believe that, besides nuclear weapons, other types of weapons of mass destruction, such as chemical and biological weapons, also pose a serious threat to humanity. The Iranian nation, which is itself a victim of chemical weapons, feels more acutely than any other nation the danger caused by the production and stockpiling of such weapons, and is prepared to do everything in its power to counter such threats.

We consider the use of such weapons as *haram* (religiously forbidden) and believe that it is everyone's duty to make efforts to secure humanity against this great disaster.

Sayyid Ali **Khamenei**

27 Farvardin 1389 (17 April A.D. 2010)

1 Jumada I, A.H. 1431

Information Circular

INFCIRC/657
Date: 15 September 2005

General Distribution
Original: English

Communication dated 12 September 2005 from the Permanent Mission of the Islamic Republic of Iran to the Agency

1. The Secretariat has received a Note Verbale dated 12 September 2005 from the Permanent Mission of the Islamic Republic of Iran, attaching a document entitled "Iranian Nuclear Policy and Activities – Complementary Information to the Report of the Director General (GOV/2005/67)".

2. As requested in the Note Verbale, the Note and its attachment are herewith circulated as an Information Circular.

Permanent Mission of the
Islamic Republic of Iran
to the United Nations and other
International Organizations in Vienna

جمهوری اسلامی ایران
نمایندگی دائم نزد دفتر ملل متحد و سازمانهای بین المللی
وین

IN THE NAME OF GOD

Verbal Note No. 350-1-17/ 1219

The Permanent Mission of the Islamic Republic of Iran to the United Nations and other International Organisations in Vienna presents its compliments to the Secretariat of the IAEA and has the honour to enclose "complimentary information to the Report of the Director General (Gov/2005/67".

The Permanent Mission of the Islamic Republic requests the Secretariat to circulate this Note with its attachments as an official INFCIRC document and make it available to the public through the IAEA website.

The Permanent Mission of the Islamic Republic of Iran to the United Nations and other International Organisations in Vienna avails itself of this opportunity to renew to the secretariat of the IAEA the assurances of its highest consideration.

Vienna, 12 September 2005

To The
International Atomic Energy Agency
Secretariat

August 2005

Madam Chair, Colleagues

We meet when the world is remembering the atomic bombings of the civilians in Hiroshima (6 August) and Nagasaki (9 August) sixty years ago. The savagery of the attack, the human suffering it caused, the scale of the civilian loss of life turning individuals, old and young, into ashes in a split second, and maiming indefinitely those who survived should never be removed from our memory. It is the most absurd manifestation of irony that the single state who caused this single nuclear catastrophe in a twin attack on our earth now has assumed the role of the prime preacher in the nuclear field while ever expanding its nuclear weapons capability.

We as members of the Non-Aligned Movement are proud to underline that none of the NPT members of the NAM rely on nuclear weapons in anyway for their security. That is not the case of many other States, who either possess nuclear weapons or are member of nuclear-armed alliances and it is such States that have taken on the self-assigned role of denying Iran its legal rights under the NPT to access the peaceful uses of nuclear technology in conformity with the Treaty's non-proliferation obligations.

Indeed, it is not only Iran – but also many members of NAM that are denied the peaceful uses of nuclear technology by some of the NPT nuclear-weapon States and their allies through the mechanisms of export controls and other denial arrangements. In 1995, they adopted the so-called "Iran clause" under which they agreed to deny nuclear technology to Iran in any circumstances.

You can then understand, why Iran after being denied nuclear technology in violation of the NPT, had no other option but to rely on indigenous efforts with precaution on full transparency and we succeeded in developing our nuclear technology. Iran is a nuclear fuel cycle technology holder, a capability which is exclusively for peaceful purposes.

The Leader of the Islamic Republic of Iran, Ayatollah Khamenei has issued the Fatwa that the production, stockpiling and use of nuclear weapons are forbidden under Islam and that the Islamic Republic of Iran shall never acquire these weapons. President Ahmadinejad, who took office just recently, in his inaugural address, reiterated that his government is against weapons of mass destruction and will only pursue nuclear activities in the peaceful domain. The leadership of Iran

IAEA
Atoms for Peace

Information Circular

INFCIRC/842
Date: 12 September 2012

General Distribution
Original: English

Communication dated 12 September 2012 received from the Resident Representative of the Islamic Republic of Iran concerning "Facts on Iran's Nuclear Policy"

1. The Director General has received a communication dated 12 September 2012 from the Resident Representative of the Islamic Republic of Iran to the Agency, enclosing a text entitled "Facts on Iran's Nuclear Policy".

2. The communication and, as requested by the Resident Representative, the text are herewith circulated for information.

In the Name of God,
the Most Gracious and the Most Merciful

Facts on
Iran's Nuclear Policy
12 September 2012

The international community has the right to know the factual situation about Iran's nuclear policy and activities. The distorted, bias information by some Western intelligence services and media with political motivation have created confusions and misunderstandings. Following are the facts on Iran's nuclear policy that has been and is being followed:

- Soon after the Revolution in 1979, late Imam Khomeini, the Founder of the Islamic Republic of Iran, in a public statement said: *".. If they continue to make huge atomic weapons and so forth the world may be pushed into destruction and major loss will afflict the nations. Everybody, wherever he is, the writers, intellectuals, scholars, and scientists throughout the world, should enlighten the people of this danger so that the masses of people will stand up vis-à-vis these two powers themselves and prevent the proliferation of these arms. ..."*

- Based on the above mentioned policy, though NPT was ratified before the Islamic Revolution in 1979, Islamic Republic of Iran did continue to be committed to it.

- The Islamic Republic of Iran was never and is not pursuing a nuclear weapon program. Since the triumph of the Islamic Revolution of Iran, the same policy based on Islamic school of thoughts has been well established.

- Declaration by the Supreme Leader of the Islamic Republic of Iran in the opening statement to the Heads of State and Government of the Non-Aligned Movement during the 16th NAM Summit in Tehran on 30 August 2012: *"The Islamic Republic of Iran considers the use of nuclear, chemical and similar weapons as a great and unforgivable sin. We proposed the idea of "Middle East free of nuclear weapons" and we are committed to it. This does not mean forgoing our right to peaceful use of nuclear power and production of nuclear fuel. On the basis of international laws, peaceful use of nuclear energy is a right of every country. All should be able to employ this wholesome source of energy for various vital uses for the benefit of their country and people, without having to depend on others for exercising this right. Some Western countries, themselves possessing nuclear weapons*

Index

A
Ahmadinejad 24, 27, 32, 35, 39, 40, 70, 72, 101, 132, 190, 199, 218
Akehurst 152, 156, 159, 210
America 26, 93, 101, 114, 125, 127, 133, 136, 214, 239

B
Bowett 97

C
Cheng 88, 207, 210
Civilians 46, 196
Consensus 20, 22, 42, 58, 192
Constitution 12, 35, 36, 58, 62, 63, 64, 65, 67, 68, 69, 73, 91, 117, 118, 192, 204
Custom 13, 24, 129, 134, 135, 160, 206, 207, 210, 211, 212, 213

D
Damato 148, 149, 150
Dinstein 152, 207
Distinction 46, 196
Duward 96

E
Edict 188, 212
Estern 166
Estoppel rule 97
Evidence 12, 13, 65, 94, 95, 96, 98

F
Fatwa 1, 11, 12, 14, 24, 25, 26, 27, 28, 29, 30, 31, 32, 33, 34, 35, 36, 37, 40, 41, 58, 63, 73, 74, 75, 109, 111, 129, 131, 132, 133, 134, 186, 188, 189, 190, 191, 200, 212
France 40, 91, 99, 103, 104, 107, 108, 110, 111, 112, 113, 116, 119, 120, 121, 122, 124, 127, 145, 171, 215

G
Governmental Decree 11, 12, 35, 37, 58, 59, 60, 61, 62, 63, 64, 65, 69, 70

H
Hadiths 11, 42, 43, 45, 47, 48, 50, 51, 53, 54, 55, 57, 58
Hanafi 55
Hanbali 12, 57
Higgins 142
Hobe 146, 208
Human Rights 31, 89, 178, 209, 212
Hygt 84

I
IAEA 31, 40, 187, 188, 190, 201
ICJ 29, 34, 36, 81, 82, 94, 109, 113, 137, 138, 142, 145, 171, 194, 195, 196, 197, 199, 213, 214, 215

Imam 27, 34, 39, 42, 47, 60, 61, 64, 67, 69, 70, 71, 72, 127, 128, 200

Integrity 13, 162

International Law Commission 18, 78, 137, 153, 217

International Organization 140, 195

Iraq 31, 202, 231

J

Judicial Authorities 13, 143

K

Kassese 179

Kelsen 169, 170, 209

Khamenei 1, 9, 24, 27, 32, 35, 39, 40, 70, 72, 101, 132, 190, 199, 218

Khomeini 1, 9, 24, 27, 32, 35, 39, 40, 70, 72, 101, 132, 190, 199, 218

Koskenniemi 174

L

Lauterpacht 80, 211

Law of evidence 12, 82

Legal Belief 13, 14, 154, 172

M

Maliki 12, 57

Mendelson 150, 151, 152, 155, 156, 157, 161, 170, 209

Meron 179, 180, 181, 209, 212

Morris 80

Mosavian 27

N

Necessity 11, 13, 14, 30, 165, 166

NPT 186, 187, 188, 189, 190, 191, 201

Nuclear Weapon 133, 201, 224

O

Obama 9, 24, 27, 32, 35, 39, 40, 70, 72, 101, 132, 190, 199, 218

Officials 13, 97, 98, 102

Omission 13, 156

P

Paris 133, 202, 207

Permanent Court 83, 85, 88, 89, 90, 92, 93, 102, 136, 157

Poisoning 12, 51

Practice 13, 14, 18, 85, 86, 87, 135, 148, 154, 158, 159, 164, 182, 207, 209, 211

Prophet 47, 48, 50, 52, 53, 55, 56, 57, 58, 60, 64, 193

Proportionality 45

Q

Quran 11, 42, 43, 57, 58, 60, 192, 193

R

Reason 42, 58, 61, 94, 192

Red Cross 146, 147, 181, 183

Reflexism 185

Refusal 13, 156

Religion 26
Roberts 174, 211
Rouhani 40

S

Shafei 56
Shia 12, 26, 47, 54, 55, 61
State 18, 26, 28, 30, 31, 35, 39, 42, 58, 65, 66, 69, 73, 93, 97, 109, 110, 111, 112, 113, 115, 116, 117, 118, 119, 120, 121, 122, 124, 125, 126, 136, 137, 139, 140, 141, 142, 144, 146, 148, 149, 150, 151, 152, 153, 154, 156, 157, 158, 160, 161, 163, 169, 170, 174, 177, 179, 181, 185, 187, 188, 190, 191, 192, 194, 196, 198, 201, 202, 203, 207, 208, 212, 213, 214, 224, 238
Straff 169
Sunnah 42, 43, 57
Sunni 12, 47, 48, 55
Supreme Leader 9, 12, 25, 29, 30, 62, 191, 225, 226, 227, 228, 229, 230, 231, 232, 233, 234, 235, 236, 237

T

Time 13, 160, 232
Truman 27, 115, 117, 119, 121, 125, 126, 162

U

UN Charter 31, 34, 35, 178, 195, 196
Uniformity 13, 162
United Nations 18, 25, 27, 40, 78, 89, 91, 93, 96, 97, 103, 106, 114, 117, 119, 120, 121, 131, 137, 141, 142, 178, 181, 187, 195, 196, 197, 213, 214, 216, 217, 224

V

Velayateh Faqih 64
Voluntarist 14, 168

W

Walden 169, 213
Watts 35, 86, 97
WMD 11, 12, 35, 39, 40, 43, 45, 47, 51, 54, 55, 133, 134, 143, 148, 164, 166, 169, 188, 189, 190, 191, 193, 198, 199, 200, 203, 204, 223
Wolfke 144, 145, 148, 149, 156, 210

www.ingramcontent.com/pod-product-compliance
Lightning Source LLC
Chambersburg PA
CBHW050629300426
44112CB00012B/1728